Norma Benghiat's family origins include Chinese, African, European and Middle Eastern elements. She was born in Kingston, Jamaica, but spent her early childhood in the old capital, Spanish Town. She was educated at St Andrew High School in Kingston. After leaving school she worked as a bank clerk and later as an accountant. She now holds a B.Sc. (Hons.) degree in social work from the University of the West Indies.

In 1973 she began publishing the 'Coalpot' series of Jamaican recipe postcards. Norma Benghiat has travelled widely in the Caribbean, North America, Europe, Japan, China, Egypt, Israel and Morocco. In 1982 she spent some time in Paris, where she gained first-hand experience in French patisserie. For six years she wrote for Air Jamaica's bi-monthly magazine, and she has also written for the *Jamaican Observer* (a local newspaper) and the now defunct Jamaican magazine *Lifestyle*.

Norma Benghiat live in Kingston, Jamaica.

# TRADITIONAL
# JAMAICAN COOKERY

## NORMA BENGHIAT

PENGUIN BOOKS

PENGUIN BOOKS

Published by the Penguin Group
Penguin Books Ltd, 27 Wrights Lane, London W8 5TZ, England
Penguin Books USA Inc., 375 Hudson Street, New York, New York 10014, USA
Penguin Books Australia Ltd, Ringwood, Victoria, Australia
Penguin Books Canada Ltd, 10 Alcorn Avenue, Toronto, Ontario, Canada M4V 3B2
Penguin Books (NZ) Ltd, 182–190 Wairau Road, Auckland 10, New Zealand

Penguin Books Ltd, Registered Offices: Harmondsworth, Middlesex, England

First published 1985
5

Copyright © Norma Benghiat, 1985
All rights reserved

Illustrations by Vana Haggerty

Printed in England by Clays Ltd, St Ives plc
Filmset in Optima/Sabon

**To Edna and Fred**

# CONTENTS

# ACKNOWLEDGEMENTS

The major part of the research material for this book was collected in 1976 and 1977 at the National Library, the Institute of Jamaica, and in a few weeks in 1980 at the main library of the University of the West Indies. I would therefore like to thank the librarians and members of staff of these two institutions for their helpfulness.

I am grateful to my sisters Blondine and Lima for their general guidance; to my mother, whose recipes and techniques have been the source of much of the contents of this book; to my husband Fred for his steadfast support; to my sister-in-law Suzy for her constant encouragement; and to Derrick Dunn of the Innswood Distillery Ltd for information on the manufacture of rum.

I am indebted to the National Library, the Institute of Jamaica, for allowing me to quote passages from *Lady Nugent's Journal (1801–1805)* and proverbs from *Jamaica Proverbs and Sayings* by Izett Anderson and Frank Cundall; to J. M. Dent & Sons Ltd and J. B. Lippincott Co. for extracts from *Voodoo Gods* by Zora Neale Hurston; to the University of North Carolina Press for quotes from Gonzalo Fernandez de Oviedo's *Natural History of the West Indies*, translated and edited by Sterling A. Stoudemire (No. 32 in the Studies in the Romance Languages and Literatures series. Copyright 1959 The University of North Carolina Press. Reprinted by permission); to Heinemann Educational Books Ltd and Sangster's Book Stores Ltd for extracts from *The Sun and the Drum* by Leonard E. Barrett; and to the Historical Society of Jamaica for permission to use extracts from the translation of *A Description of Jamaica in 1644* by J. L. Pietersz.

Finally, I wish to thank Thelma McKenzie, Elaine Brooks and Grace Edwards for typing the manuscript; Felicia Pheasant for her meticulous and sympathetic editing; and Eleo Gordon and Suzanna Zjohar of Penguin for their support.

# EQUIVALENTS CHART

Here and in the recipes, convenient equivalents are given rather than exact conversions. Cooks should follow one or other of the systems.

## LIQUIDS

| | | |
|---|---|---|
| ¼ cup | 2 fl oz | 50 ml |
| ½ cup | 4 fl oz (¼ pint) | 125–150 ml |
| 1 cup | 8 fl oz | 250 ml |
| 1 ½ cups | 12 fl oz | 350 ml |
| 2 cups | ¾ pint | 500 ml |
| 2 ½ cups | 1 pint | 600 ml |
| 3 cups | 1 ¼ pints | 750 ml |
| 4 cups (1 quart) | 1 ½ pints | 1 litre |
| 5 cups | 2 pints | 1.25 litres |
| 10 cups | 4 pints | 2.5 litres |

## SOLIDS

| | |
|---|---|
| 1 oz | 25 g |
| 2 oz | 50 g |
| 3 oz | 75 g |
| 4 oz | 100–125 g |
| 5 oz | 150 g |
| 6 oz | 175 g |
| 8 oz | 250 g |
| 1 lb | 500 g |
| 2 lb | 1 kg |
| 3 lb | 1 ¼–1 ½ kg |
| 5 lb | 2 ¼–2 ½ kg |

## EQUIVALENTS OF PRINCIPAL SOLID INGREDIENTS

| | | | |
|---|---|---|---|
| flour | 1 cup | 5–6 oz | 150–175 g |
| cornmeal | 1 cup | 6 oz | 175 g |
| white sugar | 1 cup | 8 oz | 250 g |
| brown sugar | 1 cup | 6 oz | 175 g |
| butter/margarine | 1 cup | 8 oz | 250 g |
| raisins | 1 cup | 6 oz | 175 g |
| rice | 1 cup | 7 oz | 200 g |
| red peas/gungo peas | 1 cup | 8 oz | 250 g |
| grated coconut | 1 cup | 4 oz | 125 g |

## OVEN TEMPERATURE EQUIVALENTS

| *Fahrenheit* | *Centigrade* | *Gas* | *Heat of oven* |
|---|---|---|---|
| 225°F | 110°C | ¼ | Very cool |
| 250°F | 130°C | ½ | Very cool |
| 275°F | 140°C | 1 | Cool |
| 300°F | 150°C | 2 | Cool |
| 325°F | 160°C | 3 | Moderate |
| 350°F | 180°C | 4 | Moderate |
| 375°F | 190°C | 5 | Fairly hot |
| 400°F | 200°C | 6 | Fairly hot |
| 425°F | 220°C | 7 | Hot |
| 450°F | 230°C | 8 | Very hot |
| 475°F | 240°C | 9 | Very hot |

# INTRODUCTION

Cooking was always a very important part of the daily life of my family. Among my first memories I can vividly recall Saturday morning, market day in the old capital, Spanish Town, where we lived. My mother would be up by five in the morning to arrive at the market by six. Being early, she got the pick of the fruits and vegetables and bought enough to last until the next market day.

The fruit ladies had their baskets piled high with the fruits in season. In the earlier months of the year there would be an abundance of citrus fruits – oranges, uglies, shaddock, tangerines, mandarins and grapefruits. Then there would be star apples, pawpaws, sweet and sour sops, naseberries, bananas, mangoes, avocado pears, otaheite apples, June plums, yellow coach plums, guineps and tamarinds.

The vegetables included callaloo, okra, Indian kale, cucumbers, tomatoes, lettuce and string beans. There would be yellow and St Vincent yams, Irish potatoes, cocos and dasheen, and also ginger, pimento berries, curry and annatto.

At that time there were no meat shops or supermarkets with packaged meats, so one's supply of meat for the week had to be bought at the butchers' shops in the market. The crowding of the meat stalls at times produced frayed tempers and great confusion, but it became an indelible part of the colourful scene. Beef, pork and goat were offered for sale. Chicken, ducks and pigeons were bought live. Much time was spent feeling, weighing by hand and checking to see that the chickens' craws were not over-heavy with corn.

Soon the market would be in full swing. Vendors in their starched dresses, head wraps and aprons with voluminous pockets produced a riot of colour like a hedge of variegated bougainvillea. String bags heavy with money were pulled out from the recesses of large bosoms to give change. The never-ending cries of the hand-cart men making their way through the crowd, interspersed occasionally with the hoot of truck horns or vehicles arriving with vendors bringing their produce from the country, were all part of the intensity and colour of market day.

A hand-cart man was hired to transport the shopping to the house. By 10 a.m. the last of the marketing had arrived, followed shortly by my mother and old Mother Annie, our helper. There was always an air of excitement on Saturday mornings, for in the depths of these cavernous baskets we children found some special fruit or sweet, perhaps large circles of peppermint candy with red and white stripes.

Saturday lunch was invariably the traditional one-pot meal – beef soup. I was often given the job, of which I was very fond, of cutting up the 'leggins', which was a bunch of vegetables – pieces of cho cho, turnip, carrot, pumpkin and a few sprigs of parsley – all tied together with a piece of banana bark. Shin of beef, pickled pig's tail, salt beef and the vegetables were put to boil until the meat was tender; then yams, dumplings, cocos and seasoning were added. The aroma of the beef soup permeated the house, suggesting that lunch would soon be ready.

My mother's repertoire was wide, taking into account the likes and dislikes of the large household: some did not eat chicken, others pork, others goat, so that the common standby always had to be beef. Chicken was eaten only on Sunday. Apart from beef soup and chicken which had their specific days, the menu changed from day to day. Years later I had the great pleasure of breaking with tradition, having beef soup and chicken when I liked. As pork was rarely eaten at home, almost all my knowledge of it was gained elsewhere.

My mother's excellent cooking was taken for granted. Its quality became clear only when I was exposed to other people's cooking. My father, who was Chinese, was also an excellent cook in his own right, but his influence on the cooking of the household was limited. At Double Ten or the Chinese New Year holiday, however, he became master of the kitchen.

It was not until I lived and attended high school in Kingston that I began to realize that Jamaican foods – especially those dishes that had a ring of slavery – were looked down on in some circles. Over the years, as I explored by reading and by travelling many of the cuisines of Europe and, through my Egyptian-born husband, the Middle East, I came to have a greater understanding of what my own country's cooking was all about. I felt that for too long it had gone unrecognized, and with this I turned my full attention to discovering more about Jamaican cooking.

In 1976 I started the research for this book in earnest, spending most of my mornings at the Institute of Jamaica. Later I collected additional material from the Main Library of the University of the West Indies at Mona. I gradually realized that it was necessary to cover not only contemporary Jamaican cooking, but also its roots and the influence of the Arawaks, Spanish, Jews, English, Africans, French, East Indians and Chinese. It was a revelation to realize that some of our dishes were not unique, but common to other countries, including many in the Caribbean.

I discovered from the writings of M. G. Lewis and Lady Nugent that, during the brighter years of sugar, many Europeans had a receptive attitude towards indigenous food and that creole cooking was highly thought of in some circles.

Two factors led to the denigration of creole cooking. The first was the emergence of the tourist industry (an offshoot of the banana industry), which was based on the misguided concept that Continental food was necessary to attract a rich clientele. The industry was run by the local whites, who clung to English eating habits as a form of status symbol, and by Americans.

Later, the emerging brown/black middle class, as is always the case with those newly enjoying social mobility, outwardly despised many aspects of their own culture which tied them to their past. In front of foreigners they appeared to reject indigenous food, yet they all ate creole cooking at home.

Since the departure of a great number of the middle class to other shores in recent times, these emigrants have developed a great nostalgia for their own food. Now they pay ridiculous prices for yam and other 'common' foods. The joke goes that whereas people used to make the foreign apple pie from the lowly cho cho and lime juice, some Jamaicans abroad now try to make cho cho pie from apples!

Some of the recipes in this book have never before been written down, being perhaps of peasant origin, passed on from one generation to the next by word of mouth. Some give my family's interpretation of a dish, which may vary slightly from other versions. Most of the dishes are easy to prepare, though some do need lengthy cooking. It is worth allowing food to cook slowly if you can, for although pressure cookers are at times very handy, the resultant texture and taste are never as good as those produced by cooking over a slow fire.

Although specific measurements are given, there is scope for the adventurous cook to add to or subtract from the ingredients.

As this book has been written for readers living in Jamaica as well as for those abroad, an attempt has been made to meet the needs of a wide audience. Each food or cooking term that may be unfamiliar to some readers is explained at its first main appearance in the book, and readers for whom these descriptions are superfluous are asked to be tolerant.

The system of measurements in the recipes has also been designed to cater for a variety of readers. Jamaican cooks themselves use a mixture of British and U.S. measurements, and the recipes should be easy to use for those used to working with either of these systems and for those using metrics.

A list of suppliers of West Indian produce in the U.K. will be found on p. 235.

## A SHORT HISTORY OF THE ISLAND AND ITS FOOD

The food and cooking methods of all countries reflect their history, but nowhere is this more evident than in Jamaica. Jamaican cuisine is very much the product of the contributions of various peoples who have settled in the island over the centuries, and it may therefore be useful to look briefly at its history.

As far as we know, the first inhabitants of Jamaica were the Arawak Indians who came from the lowlands of northern South America. They were peaceable people who lived in villages mainly near the coast and had little contact with the outside world. It is difficult to say how much the Arawaks brought with them in their migration and how much they found to be native to Jamaica. Many plants and animals must have been common to the whole area. In any case, their principal foods were cassava (from which they made bammies in the same way as we do today), corn, sweet potatoes, yampie, beans, callaloo, hot peppers, pimento, fish, conies, iguanas, crabs, guavas, pineapples, prickly pear and paw-paw. They also appear to have drunk cocoa.

In addition to bammies, we have retained another Arawak dish, namely the pepperpot. Its ingredients have changed over the years according to the meat and vegetables available, and the dish has become more of a soup than a stew, but it is still a link with the first inhabitants of our island.

The Arawaks certainly spit-roasted fish and meat, and may, like other Amerindians of the period, have used the barbacoa, a wooden grate standing on four forked sticks, placed over a slow fire, on which meat was cured. Our jerked pork probably dates from this time.

In 1492 Columbus took Jamaica in the name of the King of Spain, but it was not until the early years of the sixteenth century that permanent settlements were finally established. In the early years of their rule the Spaniards introduced pigs, cattle, goats and horses, and soon there were great numbers of these animals roaming the rich grazing lands of St Ann. The island became an important supplier of smoked and salted meat to Spanish ships on their way to the American mainland. In addition, lard melted down from the fat of these animals, and their hides, were exported to the other islands. 'Peel-neck' fowl, known as 'panya' fowl, is also probably of Spanish origin.

The Spaniards depended on the whole on the Indian crops for survival, but they in turn introduced a number of fruit trees and plants, such as the banana, plantain, sugar cane, lemon, lime, Seville and Valencia orange, coconut, tamarind, ginger, date palm, pomegranate, grape and fig. From other parts of the New World tropics they introduced the guinep and the naseberry.

The Spaniards learned from the Indians the method of preserving meat by smoking, but they introduced frying, which explains their need for lard, as olive oil was scarce. Our escoveitch fish is of Spanish origin too, and many of our bean and pea dishes, such as stew peas, oxtail and beans, cowfoot and beans, are reminiscent of similar Spanish dishes.

In 1655 the English were successful in occupying the island, as it was almost undefended. During the retreat some of the Spaniards fled to Cuba, and others such as Ysassi fled to the mountains, where they harassed the English for five years. The Spaniards were finally dislodged from the island in 1660, but the Portuguese Jews, who had come to Jamaica with the Spanish, preferred to remain, their number being augmented by other Jews who came to settle early during the English rule.

The Jews seem to have carried over to the English period some of the Spanish dishes, such as pea and bean dishes, which are very similar to the food of the Sephardic Jews in the Middle East. Very little written information is to be found on Jewish cooking in Jamaica, but Annie Manville Fenn, writing in 1893 about house-keeping in Jamaica, mentions the goods sold by the itinerant cake vendor and notes: 'These confections are made, I am told, by the Jewish ladies, who employ the black women as sellers.' The Jews apparently imported into Jamaica the egg plant (aubergine), and the wangla (sesame seed), from which they made caramel cakes which were once very popular, though now they are rarely seen.

Following the revolt of the slaves on St Domingue (Haiti), itself inspired by the French Revolution of 1789, a number of French émigrés arrived in Jamaica. This influx produced a period of heightened tension among the planter class, but in due course those who stayed were accepted into the social order of the day. These French émigrés may have given us our beef soup with its bunch of vegetables known as 'leggins' (possibly from 'légumes'), and perhaps also the patty.

The first Africans were brought to the island by the Spanish, who had virtually exterminated the Arawaks within fifty years of their arrival and so needed another source of labour. The importation of slaves was continued by the English. The Africans who were brought to Jamaica came from a number of different tribes, but the most dominant appear to have been the Ashanti and Fanti peoples, and then the Yoruba and Ibo peoples.

The master was obliged to give a minimum of salted meat and fish to his slaves at least once a year, and they acquired a great liking for these foods which was passed down from generation to generation and remains to this day. Apart from this meat and fish, the slaves had to grow their own food. They were given a certain amount of ground on which to grow their own provisions, and they also cultivated certain valuable crops around their huts. They grew such things as yam, pigeon (gungo) peas, okra, callaloo, corn, cocoa, coffee, calabash trees, oranges, shaddock, hot peppers, pimento, pumpkins and ackees. By 1790 the slaves were cultivating enough to be able to sell the surplus at Sunday markets in order to buy extra salted meat and fish.

The Europeans were concerned that the slaves should not develop a taste for fresh meat, and the negroes were for a while prohibited from rearing cattle. By the nineteenth century, however, the island had come to depend on them for its supplies of poultry and livestock.

Two dishes of African origin which we still know today are dokono and fufu, the method of dipping pieces of dough into soup or sauce being part of the African tradition. We still have certain African utensils, such as the yabba (an earthenware pot for slow cooking), the calabash (a gourd used as a food or water container) and the kreng kreng (a basket or wire container in which meat and fish were smoked over a kitchen fire). The huge wooden mortars in which corn, plantain and yam were pounded and coffee threshed are still to be found in rural areas.

With the abolition of slavery in the 1830s and the reluctance of the negroes to work on the plantations, West Indian planters were forced to seek new sources of labour. In order to reduce the supposed danger of having only one group from which to draw the workforce, attempts were made to lure cheap white labour. This resulted in the arrival of small numbers of Irish and German labourers. This venture proved unsuccessful, and so some Indian and a few Chinese indentured workers were brought over. Waves of immigrants such as Syrians and Jews from the Middle East also added to the growing cultural complexity of the island. These minorities have contributed a few dishes to the standard repertoire, but they have had less impact on Jamaican food as such than the major settlers.

Curry goat was probably introduced by the Indians. The English who had been in India were also fond of curry dishes, and Caroline Sullivan gives a recipe or two in her *Jamaican Cookery*

*Book* (1893), but as the white population generally looked down on goat meat it seems more likely that the dish was invented by the Indians who had settled in Jamaica. In any case, curry goat is now one of Jamaica's favourite dishes and the Indians are considered the experts in making it. They still make their own curry powders, which are much better than commercial mixtures. Other Indian foods are popular in Jamaica, but they have kept their cultural identity and are not considered as Jamaican food.

Chinese food, too, is very popular in Jamaica, and Chinese restaurants are well frequented, but the food is considered Chinese and not Jamaican.

Jamaican Syrians now eat much the same as everyone else, but one thing we have taken over from their native cuisine is Syrian bread (pitta), which is very popular in the island and can be bought in many supermarkets.

Jamaica remained British until it gained its independence in 1962. Inevitably, 300 years of British rule left an indelible mark on most aspects of Jamaican life. In terms of food, they introduced plants such as the breadfruit, otaheite apple, ackee, mango, rose apple, mandarin orange, cherimoyer, turmeric, black pepper and coffee. They imported salted and pickled provisions, mostly for the slaves, as we have seen.

Considering the long period of colonization, however, very few English dishes have remained. These include roast beef (though our version is heavily spiced and could be better described as spiced beef), and corned or salt beef. A number of our sweets do reflect a strong English influence. Our Christmas pudding, many cakes and tarts and our Easter bun are taken from the English. Jamaicans are also fond of porridge, but our porridges are sweet, spiced and flavoured, and it is not quite certain if this is an English legacy or not, because a porridge or 'pap' was made from maize by the Arawaks.

Many of the customs and words of the plantation remain with us, especially in the country areas. For instance, 'tea' is the generic name for any non-alcoholic hot drink, including coffee, cocoa or chocolate. Even fish broth is called fish tea.

As British domination has declined, so Jamaican society has come increasingly under the influence of its near neighbour, the

U.S.A., and American-style snacks or fast foods (hamburgers, fried chicken, pizzas, ice cream) vie with the more traditional patties, fish and bammies in the larger towns.

With independence has come a wish to reassess all the strands that make up present-day Jamaican culture, and a particular interest in the Jamaican people's non-European origins. A new pride in Jamaicanness is replacing the old feeling that what was Jamaican was inferior. This attitude is reflected in an increasing interest in traditional Jamaican food, and whereas the major dishes never went out of fashion, some items that were once hard to come by are again seen in the shops and on tables.

This brief survey of Jamaica's history shows how varied are the roots of Jamaican society and of our cooking. There are similarities with the food of many other countries in different parts of the globe, but the particular mixture of cultures we have known gives Jamaican cooking its originality and richness.

## A NOTE ON JAMAICAN MEAL PATTERNS

Traditional Jamaican eating patterns are rather different from those that may be familiar to some readers. Up to 150 years ago 'tea' was taken at 6 a.m. and might be an infusion, coffee or a cup of chocolate. (Breakfast is often still referred to as 'tea', especially in the country areas.) Breakfast was taken at around 8 a.m. and 'second breakfast' at midday. This last term has now disappeared. In the country areas dinner could be taken from as early as 3 p.m. to about 6 p.m., or as soon as workers returned home. (Today breakfast is from 6–8 a.m., lunch from 12 a.m. to 2 p.m., and dinner is still taken early by many, from 4 p.m. onwards.)

Breakfast was traditionally a substantial meal, consisting of a fruit such as pawpaw, followed perhaps by a banana porridge, and then a dish such as ackee and saltfish or escoveitch fish served with johnny cakes, bammies, green bananas and the like. Green tea, coffee or an infusion would be drunk. In more recent times these heavier meals have tended to be relegated to the weekend, and weekday breakfasts may follow a more international pattern with fruit or juice, a porridge or packaged cereal, and perhaps eggs and bacon.

In the past, both lunch and dinner have been big meals, but the European pattern of having several courses served one after the other is not a common feature here. Usually the main courses for both lunch and dinner are accompanied by several side dishes. Starters are not traditional, although a soup might precede the main course. On the other hand, a rich, thick soup may simply be followed by a sweet.

A traditional lunch might include such dishes as curry goat or liver and onions with yams, rice and green vegetables, followed by a custard, a pone or a cake. Dinner might be a rich soup or a stew, again served with rice, plantains, dumplings, greens, etc., and followed by the same sort of dessert as at lunch. Nowadays, however, lunch is generally a lighter affair, especially in the towns, and many people simply eat a patty or a sandwich, hamburger or hot dog. Dinner is for most people the main meal of the day.

On Sunday this pattern is reversed, with the main meal of the week being a late Sunday lunch, consisting of a meat or poultry dish accompanied by the usual range of vegetables and starches. Rice and peas and fried plantains are a must at Sunday lunch. Sunday supper is then a lighter meal.

Fruit is eaten at any time of the day and is not considered a dessert unless, for example, it is in a fruit salad or matrimony. A dessert is more often a prepared sweet – potato pone, cake or pie.

Snacks are taken any time during the day – these may be a piece of banana bread or a bun and cheese with a glass of lemonade or milk, or, under the more recent American influence, ice cream and commercially produced soft drinks.

For times of celebration or at large gatherings, the curry goat 'feed' is popular. The more affluent household will provide a buffet with many dishes.

# SPICES AND HERBS

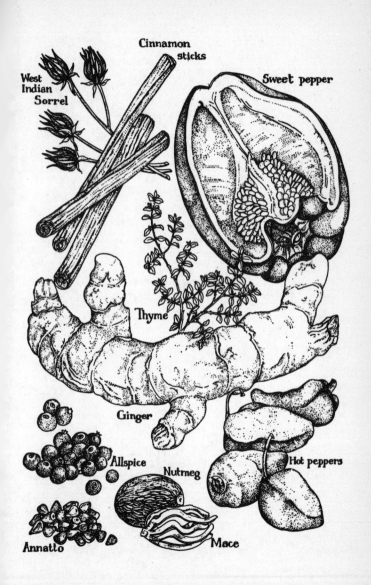

West Indian Sorrel

Cinnamon sticks

Sweet pepper

Thyme

Ginger

Allspice

Nutmeg

Hot peppers

Annatto

Mace

Jamaican food, like most food of the tropics, is highly spiced. There is probably some truth in the belief that spicing used to be a method of disguising a certain taste in meat at a time when refrigeration was unknown and all meats had to be consumed within a few days after the animal was killed. Pickled, smoked and cured meats played an important part in the diet of this period. Today, fresh hot peppers are the hallmark of Jamaican cooking. The other everyday seasonings in the household are thyme, escallion, garlic, onion, tomatoes, black pepper and salt. The seasonings used will, of course, vary according to the tastes of the household and the cook. Whatever combinations you choose, bear in mind that the use of fresh herbs and freshly ground spices can often make the difference between a good dish and an exceptional one.

Most of the important spices originating in tropical Asia, such as cinnamon, cloves, cardomom, ginger, turmeric, nutmeg and mace, were introduced into Jamaica, and some of these are now common commodities on the local market. The major spices occurring in the tropical Americas are our own pimento, vanilla and capsicums, which include both hot and sweet peppers. These were in turn introduced into the Orient and have become important ingredients in the cuisine of many far-away places.

## ANNATTO

Annatto (*Bixa orellana*) is native to the West Indies and the tropical Americas. It is now grown in many other tropical countries. The seeds, orangy-red in colour, have traditionally been used to colour and flavour various soups, stews and fish dishes. The seeds are often steeped in oil, which in turn takes the colour of the annatto. In some Spanish countries in the region it is ground and used as a spice.

Annatto is sometimes seen in markets and supermarkets. If it is not available, use saffron or turmeric.

## BLACK AND WHITE PEPPER

The first pepper plant was brought to Jamaica from the East Indies by Thomas Hibbert in 1787.

Both black and white pepper (*Piper nigrum*) are made from the berries of the pepper tree, black pepper from the dried unripe berries and white from ripe berries whose skin has been removed.

Black pepper is more aromatic and flavourful and is more useful in general cooking. It makes all the difference to a dish if the black pepper is freshly ground, for while the berries retain their flavour and aroma almost indefinitely, these deteriorate once the pepper is ground.

## CINNAMON

The sticks and leaves of the cinnamon plant (*Cinnamomum zelyanicum*) are tied into little bundles and sold in our markets. These are used to flavour 'country chocolate', puddings, porridges and other sweets; they also play an important part in the flavouring of drinks and liqueurs. The plant was introduced here by Samuel Vaughn from Ceylon in the eighteenth century.

## CURRY

Curry was possibly introduced here first by the English, who knew it through their colonization of India, and then by the East Indians who came to the island in the nineteenth century. Curry goat is the most famous of our curry dishes, followed closely by curried lobster and crab. Curry is also used to flavour our beef patties and other dishes such as gungo pea stew.

Curry powders vary from brand to brand, and one can never be sure whether the memorable flavour enjoyed today will be recaptured again. Curry powder made at home with freshly ground spices is far superior to the prepacked varieties. Here is a recipe for a good curry.

4 oz (100 g) coriander seeds, roasted and ground
4 oz (100 g) ground turmeric
1 oz (25 g) ground fenugreek
4 oz (100 g) ground ginger
4 oz (100 g) ground black pepper
1 oz (25 g) ground cardamom
1 oz (25 g) ground cinnamon

Mix all the ingredients together and store in an airtight jar.

## ESCALLION

Escallion (*Allium fistulosum*) belongs to the same family of plants as the onion, garlic and chive. It most resembles the spring onion in appearance, but its flavour is stronger. It is extensively used in Jamaican cooking, often instead of or with onion. The week's supply of this aromatic seasoning is bought in the markets in bundles in which some thyme is included.

As a substitute, use spring onion or onions.

## GINGER

The rhizome of the ginger plant (*Zingiber officinale*) is exported in its dried form to make powdered ginger. It was introduced from the Orient in 1527 by the Spaniards. Jamaica produces the finest quality ginger in the world. We use it mainly in its fresh green form to perfume our puddings, cakes, sweets and sorrel drink and to make ginger beer. Ginger tea relieves stomach ache and spasms.

## MACE

Mace is the netlike outer covering of the nutmeg. When freshly picked it is pink in colour, turning brown as it dries. Oil of mace was at one time considered valuable for the relief of insomnia. We use it for flavouring porridges and drinks.

## NUTMEG

Nutmeg is the inner kernel of the fruit of the tree *Myristica officinalis*. It is an aromatic spice, stimulating in taste. Some people have even become addicted to it! It is used mostly in the flavouring of drinks, cakes and puddings. It is kept whole, being grated as the need arises, so that the aroma is preserved.

## PEPPERS

The *Capsicum frutescens* family includes both hot and sweet peppers. These are native to the West Indies and the tropical Americas. There are many varieties of the hot pepper. When dried and ground they are sold as cayenne or chilli. Dried and ground sweet pepper becomes paprika, of which the Hungarian variety is considered to be the best.

In Jamaica, much use is made of fresh peppers, the most highly esteemed hot pepper being the 'Scotch bonnet', which has a wonderful perfume and flavour. In recent times a Scotch bonnet pepper has been developed which retains the aroma and flavour, but is not hot.

## PIMENTO (ALLSPICE)

Pimento (*Pimenta officinalis*) or Jamaica pepper, also known as allspice or the French *toute-épice*, as it is very like a mixture of nutmeg, cinnamon and cloves, is an evergreen of the myrtle family. It is indigenous to Jamaica and to a lesser extent southern Cuba, and is closely related to the bay tree and to the clove. The berries grow upon a handsome glossy-leaved tree with rough white bark. The berries mature from July to October, and are harvested while still green by breaking off the limbs bearing the berries. The berries are stripped from the branches, collected in baskets and put to dry in the sun on barbecues.

This spice has been in use in English cooking for a long time, mainly in pickles and marinades. Mention of it appears frequently in recipes of the Edwardian period. The earliest mention of pimento being exported to London occurs in 1601, when a drug made from the berries of 'a certain tree of the myrtle family' was given to a London druggist, but it was a regular item on the Spanish bills of trade even earlier than that, and of course it was used by the Arawaks. I have not, however, been able to trace how it came to be used in such abundance in the Levant, but perhaps it reached the countries bordering the Mediterranean via Spain. We have had a steady trade with Russia, where pimento is used in the cooking of the area near the Black Sea.

Pimento is an important ingredient of some of our dishes, especially jerked pork and escoveitch fish, and it is also used in pickles, marinades, soups and stews. Pimento liqueur is made from the ripe, purplish berries.

## TURMERIC

Turmeric (*Curcuma longa*) is a member of the ginger family. It is known locally as tumeric, and is the main ingredient of curry powder. It can be used as a substitute for curry or saffron, mainly for the colouring effect, though turmeric has its own mild and delightful flavour.

## VANILLA

The pods of the climbing orchid, *Vanilla planifolia*, native to Mexico, provide us with commercially produced vanilla. We use it in the flavouring of puddings, cakes, ice creams, sweets in general and some drinks. The vine was first brought here from South America by a Mr Thame in 1787.

## HERBS

Thyme is perhaps our most cherished herb. It is sold in its fresh form, tied in little bundles or included in a bunch of escallion. We have two varieties – the broad-leafed 'French thyme' and the more popular small-leaved thyme which is more fragrant. Our other herbs, sweet basil (bawsley) and mint of various kinds as well as fever grass, are used more often to make teas and infusions than in cooking. These teas are included in a separate chapter, Medicinals and Herb Teas (p. 225).

# APPETIZERS

The question invariably arises – should one spend a lot of time preparing appetizers to hand round before a dinner party or should one concentrate on the main dishes? My answer is that if my main courses are time-consuming in their preparation, I spend less time on appetizers. On the other hand, easily prepared main courses such as steaks and grills leave me more time to do as I wish.

As in Jamaica we tend not to have a European-style first course, there is perhaps more room for appetizers to be eaten before the meal. The drinking of rum, a naturally sweet alcohol, makes salty titbits particularly popular.

Unusual appetizers always please, especially if they are home-made, and if dinner is to be served late, your guests will doubly welcome these tasty morsels. Whatever you do, be sure that your appetizers suggest that better things are to come!

## ACKEE AND SALTFISH APPETIZER

This is quite a filling appetizer, particularly appropriate if you are serving a light main course.

Prepare the ackee and saltfish recipe on p. 77. Line some muffin tins with slices of bread, their crusts removed. Using 1 slice of bread for each muffin hole, press the bread into the holes (it will not fit exactly). Fill each with ackee and saltfish, sprinkle some grated cheese on top, and bake for 10 minutes in a hot oven.

## AVOCADO DIP

2 avocados
1 stalk escallion, chopped
1 tablespoon vinegar *or* lime juice

2 oz (50 g) chopped ham
  (optional)
½ teaspoon salt

Halve the avocados and scoop out all the flesh. Either put all the ingredients in a blender, or press the flesh of the avocados through a sieve with a wooden spoon to get it very smooth. Then add the other ingredients. If you are using the ham, omit the salt. Serve the dip with crackers or plantain chips. Enough for 6.

## CODFISH BALLS

6 potatoes
½ lb (250 g) salt cod
1 tablespoon butter

hot pepper, finely chopped
1 egg, beaten
oil

Peel the potatoes and boil them in water with the salt cod until the potatoes are tender. Drain. Remove the skin and bones from the fish and shred it, then pound it in a mortar until it is fine in texture. Mash the potatoes and add the butter, hot pepper, pounded fish and beaten egg. The mixture should be firm enough to mould into little balls – add a little flour if it is not holding together. Fry the fish balls in hot oil and drain them on kitchen paper. Serve hot. Enough for 6.

## PICKLED RED HERRING

2 lb (1 kg) smoked red herring
1 onion, chopped
½ cup (¼ pint, 150 ml) vinegar

2 hot peppers, chopped
a few pimento berries

First remove the skin from the fish. To do this, wrap the fish loosely with some newspaper and set it alight, allowing the paper to burn on both sides. The skin will now come off easily. Discard the head, remove all the bones, and shred the fish into small pieces. Place in a bowl and add the chopped onion, vinegar, hot peppers and pimento. Mix well and bottle. It will keep indefinitely. Serve with crackers or thin squares of bread.

# SOLOMON GUNDY

2 lb (1 kg) pickled shad
½ lb (250 g) pickled herring
½ lb (250 g) pickled mackerel
2 onions
2 hot peppers, Scotch bonnet if
  possible, chopped

½ cup (¼ pint, 150 ml) salad oil
12 pimento berries
vinegar

Place the shad, herring and mackerel in a large bowl. Cover them with cold water and leave to soak for at least 4 hours to get rid of the excess salt. Discard this water and add enough boiling water to cover the fish completely. Leave for 5 minutes, then again discard the water.

Remove the skin and heads from the fish, and as many of the bones as possible. Either put the flesh of the fish through a food mill with the onions and hot peppers, or chop the fish, onions and peppers very finely. Mix very well. Add the oil, the whole pimento berries and enough vinegar to make a paste. Store in sterilized jars. It will keep indefinitely. Serve on crackers or thin slices of bread.

If shad is unavailable, use increased quantities of the other fish.

# STAMP AND GO

The name 'Stamp and go' is often attributed to its fiery nature. But Caroline Sullivan, who describes it in *Jamaica Cookery Book* (1893) as a mixture of flour and cornmeal with the usual spicing, says that 'The country people as they travel stop at the wayside and buy these with a slice of bread for a trifle. Hence the name.'

½ lb (250 g) salt cod
3 cups (1 lb, 500 g) flour
1 teaspoon baking powder
  (optional)
3 stalks escallion, chopped

2 hot peppers, chopped
½ small tomato, chopped
½ teaspoon thyme leaves
oil

Soak the fish in water for 30 minutes, then remove the bones and skin and shred the fish finely. Place the flour in a bowl, and add the baking powder, escallion, hot peppers, tomato and thyme and just enough water to make a soft sticky batter. Make fritters of the desired size by dropping the mixture from a spoon into medium hot oil and fry them until they are golden brown. Drain them on absorbent paper and serve them hot. Enough for 4.

## CHIPS

Home-made chips are far tastier than the mass-produced ones that you find in the supermarkets. They are worth the effort of making them at home.

## COCONUT CHIPS

2 dry coconuts                                   salt

Break the shells of the coconut by hitting them with a heavy implement such as a hammer. Cut the coconut flesh into several pieces, then slice thinly. Salt the chips and either grill them, turning them over as they brown, or toast them in a moderate oven, turning them over once.

## PLANTAIN AND BANANA CHIPS

Use green bananas and plantains. Remove the skins, slice into thin rounds and place in some salted water for 10–15 minutes. Dry them thoroughly. Fry the chips in lots of clean hot oil until they are crisp. Drain on absorbent paper, sprinkle with salt, and store in airtight jars. They make excellent accompaniments for dips.

# BREADFRUIT CHIPS

1 green breadfruit                    oil
salted water

Peel the breadfruit. Cut it in two from top to bottom, then cut each half into several pieces. Remove the heart or core and cut the flesh into thin slices. Put these into salted water for 15 minutes, then dry them and fry in plenty of clean hot oil. Drain on absorbent paper and sprinkle with salt. Store as in the previous recipe.

# SOUPS

Jamaican soups are thick and rich. The stock is made from shin of beef or soup meat, as we call it, pig's tail and salt beef. To this stock various vegetables are added: callaloo, pumpkin, carrots, turnips, cho chos, peas and beans, depending on what the soup is to be. The soups are subtly seasoned with escallion, fresh thyme, occasionally a few grains of our pimento, and hot pepper. Soups are often served as one-pot meals, with the addition of yams, cocos and dumplings, but if a soup is to be served as a first course, it is best to use very small quantities of these.

The enterprising cook need not worry about shortages of imported pickled meats – recipes for some of these will be found in the chapter on Curing and Pickling (p. 215).

## PEPPERPOT SOUP

This is almost certainly the most famous of our soups. It is probably of Arawak origin, though it seems to have been more of a stew in those days. It is still prepared in the Amerindian way in Guyana, but in Jamaica it has changed over the years under the influence of cooks of different cultures. The ingredients have varied according to what has been available, and the dish has become more of a soup.

In the Arawaks' time, the pepperpot was said often to be generations old, as each day it was replenished with fresh meat, vegetables and water. The principal ingredients were small game animals, callaloo, and cassareep as a preservative. Cassareep is made from the highly poisonous juice of the bitter cassava, which is pressed from the grated cassava in the process of making cassava bread. The prussic acid in the juice is neutralized by boiling, and the juice is left for a few days until it becomes vinegary. The pepperpot was flavoured with hot peppers and, in Jamaica, pimento.

By the nineteenth century, the pepperpot of the rich had become a rather different dish. Lady Nugent notes in her journal of 11 March 1802:

There was also a black crab pepper-pot, for which I asked the receipt. It is as follows:

A capon stewed down, a large piece of beef and another of ham, also stewed to a jelly; then six dozen of land crabs, picked fine, with their eggs and fat, onions, peppers, ochra, sweet herbs, and other vegetables of the country, cut small; and this well stewed, makes black crab pepper-pot.

But pepperpot had not become solely a dish for the wealthy. M. G. Lewis, in *Journal of a West Indian Proprietor* (1834), says: 'The slaves on the other hand had to make their pepperpot with saltfish.'

The pepperpot we know in Jamaica today shows a clear West African influence. The cassareep has been left out somewhere along the line, although it was used in parts of St James until fairly recently.

The callaloo soup of the Eastern Caribbean resembles our pepperpot in many ways, but dasheen leaves, similar to our Indian kale, form the main vegetable ingredient, replacing the callaloo which is often referred to as 'spinach'. (Those living abroad could use spinach instead of callaloo and Indian kale for this recipe.)

| | |
|---|---|
| ½ lb (250 g) callaloo | ½ lb (250 g) each yellow yam and |
| 12 okras | coco, peeled and sliced |
| ½ lb (250 g) Indian kale leaves | 2 stalks escallion, crushed |
| 12 cups (5 pints, 2.75 litres) water | 1 sliced hot pepper, seeds removed |
| ½ lb (250 g) pig's tail *or* salt beef | black pepper |
| ½ lb (250 g) shin of beef | |
| 3 cups (1¼ pints, 750 ml) coconut milk | |

Wash thoroughly and chop finely the callaloo, okras and Indian kale leaves. Put them to boil in the water with the pig's tail or salt beef and the shin of beef for 2 hours, or until the meats are tender.

Add the coconut milk (made by adding water to 1 grated coconut, then pressing through a sieve), yam and coco, escallion, hot pepper and a little black pepper. Add more water if necessary, though the soup should be fairly thick in consistency. Simmer for a further 30 minutes. Enough for 4–6.

## ACKEE SOUP

10 cups (4 pints, 2.5 litres) water
1 lb (500 g) shin of beef
½ lb (250 g) salt beef *or* pig's tail
ackees from 2 dozen ripe open
  pods

1 sprig thyme
2 stalks escallion, crushed
2–3 slices hot pepper
black pepper

Make a stock with the water, shin of beef and salt beef or pig's tail. In the meantime boil the ackees in some lightly salted water until tender; then drain, crush them with a fork, and add them to the prepared stock. Season with the thyme, escallion, hot pepper and a little black pepper. Adjust the seasoning before serving; because of the addition of the salt beef, the soup should not need salt. Enough for 4.

## COLD AVOCADO SOUP

3 avocado pears
2 stalks escallion, finely chopped
1 tablespoon lime juice

4 cups (1½ pints, 1 litre) milk
salt
pepper

Scoop out the flesh of the avocados, place it in a bowl, and mash it to a purée with a fork. Add the escallion and lime juice and mix well, then gradually add the milk, beating constantly. Add salt and pepper to taste. Alternatively, place the avocados, escallion, lime juice and milk in a blender and mix for a minute or two, then add salt and pepper to taste. Keep the soup chilled until it is to be served. Enough for 4.

## BEEF SOUP

There is a strong suspicion that this soup was introduced by the French émigrés from Haiti in the nineteenth century. For some reason or other, it became the soup that was cooked for Saturday lunch.

When I was a child, one frequently saw bunches of fresh

vegetables, consisting of pieces of pumpkin, cho cho, carrot and turnip and a sprig of parsley, and tied with banana bark, on sale in the market. This bunch of vegetables was known as 'leggins', which Cassidy says is probably a corruption of the French word '*légumes*'. A Martiniquan whom I recently had the pleasure of meeting described the bunch of vegetables that they use for soup and it is very similar to our leggins. They call it '*légumes de soupe*'.

3 carrots, diced
1 cho cho
1 lb (500 g) West Indian pumpkin
2 turnips, diced
10–12 cups (4–5 pints, 2.5–3 litres) water
2 lb (1 kg) shin of beef
½ lb (250 g) salt beef *or* pig's tail
3 cups (1 lb, 500 g) flour for dumplings

½ lb (250 g) yam
½ lb (250 g) coco *or* green breadfruit
1 clove garlic
2 stalks escallion
1 sprig thyme
3 slices hot pepper
black pepper
12 pimento berries

Cut the carrots, cho cho, pumpkin and turnips into small pieces and put them to boil in the water with the shin of beef and the salt beef or pig's tail. When the pot starts to boil, turn the heat to a moderate temperature. In 1½–2 hours the meat should be tender and the vegetables almost dissolving. Add more water if the liquid is greatly reduced.

Make dumplings with the flour (see pumpkin soup, p. 47) and throw them into the soup with the peeled yam and cocos or breadfruit. Crush the garlic and escallion and add to the pot with the thyme and hot pepper. Sprinkle in about ½ teaspoon of black pepper and a little salt if necessary – though this will be unlikely because of the addition of the salted meat. Add the pimento berries. The soup should be ready as soon as the yam and coco or breadfruit are cooked. Enough for 4–5.

## COCONUT SOUP

1 lb (500 g) shin of beef
2 small cocos, cut into small
  pieces
10–12 cups (4–5 pints, 2.5–3
  litres) water
2 stalks escallion *or* spring onions,
  crushed

1 sprig fresh thyme
½ teaspoon black pepper
2–3 slices hot pepper (optional)
2½ cups (1 pint, 600 ml) coconut
  milk (see p. 135)

Put the shin of beef and the cocos to boil in the water. When the meat is tender (approximately 2 hours) add the escallion, thyme, black pepper and a slice or two of hot pepper if you like. Pour in the coconut milk and simmer for a few minutes, then adjust the seasoning and serve hot. Enough for 4–5.

## CONCH SOUP

The somewhat rubbery flesh of this large mollusc, whose beautiful shell is sold to tourists along the north coast, is put to good use in this excellent soup.

2 lb (1 kg) conch meat
juice of 1 lime
10–12 cups (4–5 pints, 2.5–3
  litres) water
1 cho cho, diced
3 Irish potatoes *or* cocos, peeled
  and cut in small pieces

1 sprig fresh thyme
2 stalks escallion *or* spring onions,
  crushed
1 whole hot pepper
3 slices hot pepper
salt
black pepper

Wash the conch meat thoroughly to get rid of all sand and grit. Squeeze the lime juice over the meat and rub it in with your fingers. Cut the meat into small cubes and put it to boil in water until tender (approximately 2 hours).

When the meat is cooked, add the cho cho, Irish potatoes or cocos, thyme, escallion, whole hot pepper and sliced hot pepper. Add salt to taste and a little black pepper. Bring the soup to the boil again, then turn down the heat and simmer until the vegetables are tender. Before serving remove the whole pepper without crushing it. Serves 4–5.

## OXTAIL SOUP

| | |
|---|---|
| 2 lb (1 kg) oxtail, jointed | 2 stalks escallion, crushed |
| 10–12 cups (4–5 pints, 2.5–3 litres) water | 1 sprig fresh thyme |
| | 1 whole hot pepper |
| 3 cocos, peeled and sliced | 3 slices hot pepper |
| ½ lb (250 g) yellow yam *or* other hard yam, peeled and sliced | black pepper |
| | salt |

Put the oxtail and water in a large pot and bring to the boil. Reduce the heat to medium and allow the oxtail to cook until it is tender, almost falling off the bones. This should take about 2 hours.

Add more water if the liquid has been considerably reduced, and bring to the boil once again. Lower the heat then add the cocos, yam, escallion, thyme, whole and sliced pepper, ½ teaspoon of black pepper and salt to taste. You can add dumplings (see pumpkin soup, p. 47) or some vegetables as well if you wish. Simmer for a further 15 minutes or until the cocos and yam are tender when tested with a fork. Before serving, remove the whole pepper, taking care not to crush it. Serves 4–5.

## FISH TEA

In Jamaica, the word 'tea' is used to describe any non-alcoholic drink. This is a legacy of the days of the plantations, when certain words and customs passed into the local repertoire.

Nothing is more enjoyable than to have a bowl of this hot soup, made from freshly caught fish, in one of the fishing villages on the coast.

| | |
|---|---|
| 8 cups (3½ pints, 2 litres) water | 2 stalks escallion, crushed |
| 2 lb (1 kg) fish heads or bony fish | 1 whole hot pepper, Scotch bonnet if possible |
| 6 green bananas, peeled and cut into small pieces | 3 slices hot pepper |
| 1 tomato, chopped | salt |
| 1 sprig thyme | black pepper |

Place the water and fish in a large pot and bring to the boil, then cover the pot and reduce the heat to medium. Cook the fish for 30 minutes, then strain the stock. Remove all the flesh from the bones, return this to the stock, and add the bananas, tomato, thyme, escallion and whole and sliced hot pepper. Bring to the boil again, then simmer until the bananas are tender. If the soup is too thick add some more water, then add salt and pepper to taste. Remove the whole pepper, without breaking it, and serve the broth very hot. Enough for 4.

## PUMPKIN SOUP

2 lb (1 kg) shin of beef
½ lb (250 g) salt beef or pig's tail
2 lb (1 kg) pumpkin, diced
10–12 cups (4–5 pints, 2.5–3 litres) water
1 lb (500 g) yellow yam or other hard yam
2 cocos
1½ cups (½ lb, 250 g) flour for dumplings

1 whole hot pepper, Scotch bonnet if possible
3 slices hot pepper
1 sprig thyme
2 stalks escallion, crushed
1 clove garlic
black pepper

Place the shin of beef, salt beef or pig's tail, diced pumpkin and water in a large pan. Bring to the boil, then reduce the heat and cook until the meat is tender and the pumpkin almost disintegrating. Mash the pumpkin further with a fork if necessary, then throw in the peeled yam and cocos and the dumplings. (To make the dumplings take the flour, add a little salt, and make a firm ball with the addition of a little water. You can make either round dumplings or tiny elongated ones.) Add the hot pepper slices and whole hot pepper (be careful not to let it break), together with the thyme, escallion, garlic and a little black pepper. Salt should not be necessary because of the addition of the salt beef or pig's tail. Simmer for a further 15 minutes or until the yam and cocos are tender. Before serving, remove the thyme and the whole pepper, taking care not to crush it. Enough for 4–5.

## TURTLE SOUP

Turtles used to be found in fair quantities around our coasts, feeding on turtle grass. The turtle capital, however, was the Cayman Islands, where they were found in great abundance. During the seventeenth century, sloops from Cayman used to arrive at Port Royal filled with turtles which were then taken to Port Royal's turtle market. At this time turtle meat was the staple food of poor whites. In recent years it has become scarce, and it is not often seen for sale in Kingston.

Turtles are very meaty and the flesh has the texture of veal.

| | |
|---|---|
| 2 lb (1 kg) turtle meat, cubed | 1 sprig thyme |
| ½ lb (250 g) salt beef | 12 pimento berries |
| 3 stalks escallion, crushed | 3–4 slices hot pepper |
| 10–12 cups (4–5 pints, 2.5–3 litres) water | black pepper |
| 2 tomatoes, chopped | salt |

Put the turtle meat, salt beef and escallion in a large pan and add the water. Bring to the boil, then reduce the heat and simmer until the meats are tender (approximately 1½ hours). Add the chopped tomatoes, thyme, pimento berries, hot pepper slices and black pepper. Add more water if necessary and taste for salt. Let it simmer for another 5 minutes, then remove the thyme and serve immediately. Enough for 4–5.

## GUNGO PEAS SOUP

December and January are the peak months for the gungo pea crop. No Christmas or New Year would be the same without rice and peas made with gungo peas. The bone from the Christmas ham is usually reserved for the grand gungo peas soup, which heralds the end of the festive season. It is often with nostalgia that we empty our cups to the last drop.

The gungo pea is known by various other names, including congo and pigeon pea. The plant, a hardy shrub, appears to have been introduced to the West Indies from Africa.

3 cups (1½ lb, 750 g) green gungo
  peas
1 ham bone *or* ½ lb (250 g) salt
  beef
2 lb (1 kg) shin of beef
10–12 cups (4–5 pints, 2.5–3
  litres) water
1 lb (500 g) yellow yam *or* other
  hard yam, peeled and cut in
  small pieces

3 cocos, peeled and quartered
dumplings made from ½ lb (250 g)
  flour (see pumpkin soup, p. 47)
1 whole hot pepper
3 slices hot pepper
1 sprig thyme
1 clove garlic, crushed
2 stalks escallion, crushed
black pepper
salt

Clean the peas of any grit, wash them, and put them in a large pan
with the ham bone or salt beef, the shin of beef and the water.
Bring to the boil, then reduce the heat and cover the pan.

When the meats and peas are tender, after approximately 2
hours, add the yam, cocos and dumplings. Bring the pot to the boil
again, and season the soup with the whole and sliced hot pepper,
thyme, garlic and escallion. Add a little black pepper, and salt if
necessary. Simmer for about 15 minutes, or until the yam and
cocos are soft. Before serving remove the thyme and the whole hot
pepper, taking care not to break it. Enough for 4–5.

## RED PEAS SOUP

Red kidney beans are the most popular pulses. In Jamaica they are
known as red peas.

2 cups (1 lb, 500 g) red peas
2 lb (1 kg) shin of beef
½ lb (250 g) salted pig's tail *or*
  salt beef
10–12 cups (4–5 pints, 2.5–3
  litres) water
1 lb (500 g) yellow yam *or* other
  hard yam, peeled and cut in
  small pieces
2–3 cocos, peeled and cut in small
  pieces

1½ cups (½ lb, 250 g) flour for
  dumplings (see pumpkin soup,
  p. 47)
1 whole hot pepper
3 slices hot pepper
1 clove garlic, crushed
2 stalks escallion, crushed
1 sprig thyme
black pepper
salt

Put the peas and meats in a large pan with the water and bring to the boil. Reduce the heat, cover, and allow to cook until the meats are tender. This should take about 2 hours. Crush some of the peas with a large spoon or fork, then add the yam, cocos and dumplings. Season the soup with the whole and sliced hot pepper, garlic, escallion, thyme and a little black pepper. Cook until the yam and cocos are soft, adding more water if necessary. Taste for salt. Before serving, remove the thyme and the whole pepper. You must take care not to break or cut the pepper when you are stirring the pot. Enough for 4–5.

## JONGA SOUP

Jongas or jangas are crayfish found in our rivers and streams, where they live under the rocks and stones. They are extremely difficult to catch. They are excellent plainly boiled, stewed or made into this tasty soup.

| | |
|---|---|
| 2 dozen live jongas | 3 stalks escallion, crushed |
| 8 cups (3½ pints, 2 litres) water | 3–4 slices hot pepper |
| 1 small tomato, chopped | black pepper |
| 1 sprig thyme | salt |

Wash the jongas thoroughly under running water to get rid of all sand and grit. Put them to boil in the water for 30 minutes, then remove them from the pan and pound them in a mortar, shells included. Return the pounded jongas to the stock in the pot, stir well, and leave to simmer for a further 10 minutes. Strain the broth to remove the shells, then put the broth back on the heat. Add the tomato, thyme, escallion, hot pepper, a little black pepper and salt to taste. Simmer for a further 5 minutes or so. Serve very hot with hot rolls. Enough for 4.

# FUFU

One of the dishes that survived the middle passage and is still familiar to many Jamaicans, especially those in the country areas, is fufu. It is said to be a Fanti word used often among the people of the Cape Coast.

Leonard Barrett, in his book *The Sun and the Drum* (1976), mentions that in West Africa, and especially Ghana, the word 'fufu' is used for the combination of yam, plantain and cassava, boiled and pounded into a dough, which is used in soups. The dough is worked into small pieces with the fingers, dipped into a soup or a sauce and then eaten. We now use the word 'fufu' for the whole dish.

This version is more of a sauce than a soup.

12 Indian kale leaves
1 lb (500 g) callaloo
12 okras, chopped
6 flower buds of the West Indian
    pumpkin vine (optional)
10 cups (4 pints, 2.5 litres) water
2 lb (1 kg) shin of beef

½ lb (250 g) salt beef
2 lb (1 kg) yam *or* green plantain
1 sprig thyme
2 stalks escallion, crushed
3–4 slices hot pepper (optional)
12 pimento grains

Tie the kale, callaloo, okra and flower buds in a bundle, and put them to boil in the water with the shin of beef and salt beef. When the greens are cooked, remove them from the pot and chop them very fine. Put the chopped greens back into the soup, and continue to cook until the meats are tender. At this point add the peeled yam or plantain. When the latter is cooked, pound it in a mortar, make small balls with the mixture, and set aside to keep warm.

Season the soup with the thyme, escallion, hot pepper and a few pimento grains. If the soup is too liquid, reduce it by rapid boiling until it is very thick, like a sauce. You should need no salt because of the addition of the salt beef. The fufu should take about 2 hours to cook in all.

The dish is eaten by using the fingers to dip the balls in the sauce. It is very difficult to give precise quantities for this recipe as these depend entirely on the individual's taste, but one must get the consistency of the sauce right.

# VEGETABLES
# AND PULSES

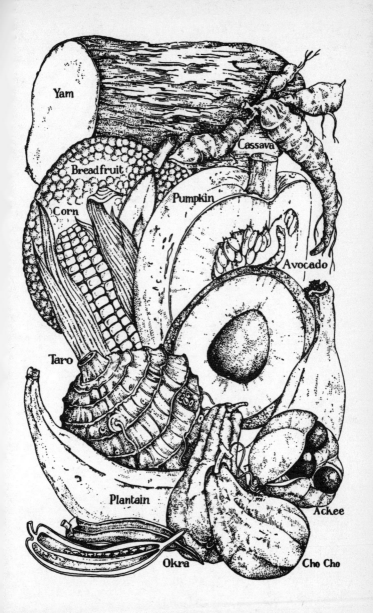

# ✳ VEGETABLES

Many of the vegetables we enjoy today in Jamaica and often consider to be our very own, such as yams, ackees, green bananas, plantains, breadfruit and potatoes, are not native to the island but were introduced at one time or another by one of the many peoples who have lived here. Some, however, have been here much longer and were either found growing on the island by the Arawaks or brought by them in their migration from South America. Callaloo, for instance, was one of the important ingredients in the Arawak pepperpot, corn was grown and made into bread, and cassava or manioc was their staple food. Other tubers such as sweet potato also had an important place in the Indians' diet.

We know that beans were cultivated by the Arawaks at the time of the Spanish discovery of Jamaica, for Columbus describes them, but we are not able to conclude from his description what species of bean they were. They may have been the common brown bean (*Phaseolus vulgaris*) which has been found in many graves from North America southwards to Peru and Argentina.

With our native vegetables as well as those introduced by successive settlers, we now have a rich and wide variety for the cook to make use of.

Before the supermarket boom of the fifties, the traditional source of the weekly supply of fruit and vegetables was the Saturday market, though in cases of emergency it was the itinerant vendor who filled the gap. Each vendor had his or her particular cry, often only intelligible to the initiated. These vendors would sell starch, fish, fruit, vegetables, yams, wood and coal, empty bottles, sweets and cakes, crabs and booby eggs.

Now we find many fruit and vegetable shops sprinkled here and there in the towns, but they lack the bustle and colour of the open market where one can choose from the freshly picked fruit and vegetables at leisure. This perhaps explains the success of the vendors or 'higglers' who are now to be found in increasing numbers in the car parks of our plazas (or shopping centres), displaying an attractive selection of fresh produce and weighing them on hand-held scales for passing customers.

Preceding the recipes is a descriptive list of the common vegetables used in our cooking.

## ✻PROVERBS✻

Far pass (i.e. long journey) mek okra 'pwoil (spoil).

Grass callalu grow whe' him nature take.

De more you chop breadfruit root de more him spring.

If plantain ben know say him neck gwine bruk,
him nebber would a shoot.

## ACKEE

It is believed that the ackee, *Blighia sapida* (named in honour of Captain Bligh of the *Bounty*), was brought to the islands by enslaved West Africans. By 1798 it was to be found as an exotic plant in the garden of Mr East at Liguanea. The fleshy yellow part or aril, which we eat, was never consumed in its native land. It is reputed that the seeds were beaten to a pulp and used as an aid in fishing. The pulp would be thrown in the river where it acted as a narcotic on the fish, which could be collected as they floated to the surface of the water.

The tree is quite beautiful with its glossy leaves and scarlet, pear-shaped pods, which when ripe split open to reveal usually three yellow-fleshed fruit, each with a glossy black seed.

The unripe ackee contains a high concentration of a poisonous substance called hypoglycine. It must be picked for consumption at the stage when the pods split open. At this stage the hypoglycine content is very low.

When preparing ackees for cooking, be sure to remove the pink membrane found in the crack of the yellow edible part, as well as the seed. It is also advisable to discard the water in which the ackees have been boiled.

Tinned ackees are exported and can be purchased from shops selling West Indian produce.

## AVOCADO

Avocados (*Persea americana*) or 'pears' as we call them, are native to the tropical Americas. They were once called 'midshipman's butter' or 'poor man's butter'. We have round pears like the large, thick-fleshed 'simmonds', and long-necked, 'alligator' pears. They are either green- or purple-skinned. Our pears are not only more attractive than those on sale in Europe, they also have so much more flavour that they seem like a different species.

Pears are a passion with us. We usually serve them sliced, with a sprinkling of salt, as an accompaniment to a main course or as a snack. They are also eaten with sweet breads and buns.

Avocados make a delicious starter, stuffed with shrimps or lobster and freshly made mayonnaise, or served with a simple vinaigrette sauce (made with the juice of half a lime, salad oil, salt and black pepper). These are not, however, Jamaican recipes.

## BANANA

The banana and its cousin, the plantain, are of the Musa genus, hybrids of the species M. *acuminata colla* and M. *balbisiana colla*.

The banana is indigenous to the Old World tropics and was brought to the Sudan and Morocco by Arabs trading in ivory and slaves. The Portuguese took it to the Guinea Coast of West Africa (1469–74), then from there to the Canary Islands in 1482, and it was from the Canaries that the plant was carried to the New World.

Some twenty-seven varieties are known in Jamaica. The 'Gros Michel', on which the Jamaican banana industry was established, was brought to the island from Martinique by Jean François Pouyat, a botanist, in 1835; this variety was called 'martinicks' by the peasants. Unfortunately the 'Gros Michel' was susceptible to the Panama disease, which almost wiped out this variety. The 'Lacatan', resistant to the disease, has now replaced the 'Gros Michel'.

The banana is eaten in the unripe state as a staple, and made into chips.

## BREADFRUIT

We know of the famous mutiny on the *Bounty* and of the ship's captain, William Bligh, but less well known is the purpose of that ill-fated voyage, which was to procure from the South Pacific breadfruit plants which were to be planted in the West Indies. The fruit of this plant was to form a cheap source of food for the slaves. On his second voyage in 1793 Bligh was successful, and he arrived in Jamaica on H.M.S. *Providence* with 347 healthy plants. It was not until a generation later, however, that the slaves touched the fruit.

The breadfruit (*Artocarpus communis*) is a beautiful, tall tree with large, glossy, heavily serrated and ribbed leaves. The fruit, borne usually in two crops per year, is round, sometimes weighing as much as 4 lb (2 kg). In its immature state it is boiled or added to soups. The mature but not ripe fruit is roasted or fried. The blossoms are also made into a preserve. The most esteemed variety is the yellow heart.

## CALLALOO

*Amaranthus viridis* was first recorded by Sloane in 1696 as calalu (*Caruru brasilionsibus*, which suggests its possible origin). The name has been spelled in several different ways.

It is a vegetable like spinach, and is one of the main ingredients in the Jamaican pepperpot soup (do not confuse this with the Eastern Caribbean's callaloo soup, which is made from the leaves of the dasheen plant, *Colocasia esculenta*).

## CASSAVA

The cassava (*Manihot utilissima*) or manioc is native to the West Indies and Central America, whence it was introduced to the East and to Africa. From the earliest times the root has been an important form of food.

The tubers are shaped like hands with fat fingers. The skin is rough, brown, and covered with a network of fine veins. The flesh is white.

There are two distinct kinds of cassava, the bitter and the sweet. Bitter cassava contains hydrocyanic or prussic acid, so the roots must be cooked before they can be used for food. The bitter cassava is the kind chiefly used in the production of starch. Sweet cassava is most commonly boiled and eaten as a vegetable. The principal sweet variety can easily be distinguished from the bitter by a characteristic yellow colour when boiled, and generally the sweet possesses a less acid smell when cut open.

From both bitter and sweet cassava is made the original Indian bread known as the bammy (see p. 120).

## CHO CHO

The cho cho (*Sechium edule*), also called chayote, bironne and christophene, grows on a luxuriant vine whose leaves resemble those of the cucumber, though they are much larger. Both are members of the gourd family. It is also known as custard marrow, vegetable pear and pepinella. It is a native of Mexico and the Antilles and is now grown in many hot countries. The fruit resembles a large pear and can be green or white with deep ribbings. The outer skin is usually covered with sharp spines.

In Jamaica, the cho cho is either boiled and served as an accompaniment to a meat dish or included in soups and stews. It is also used in the making of pickles, and with the addition of some lime juice is a very good substitute for apple in tarts and pies.

## COCOS

The coco (also known as taro and tannia) is a tuberous perennial of the Colocasia genus. It has large handsome leaves and is grown in nearly all tropical countries. It is native to the Pacific region. It is a starchy tuber, eaten in place of or in conjunction with other starches such as rice, potatoes and so on. It is usually boiled or added to soups. Coco is very similar to dasheen, a member of the same family.

## CORN

Maize or Indian corn (*Zea mays*) is indigenous to the tropical Americas. It is eaten on the cob, grilled or boiled in seasoned water. One of the great treats for travellers on the road from the south to the north coast of Jamaica is to stop on Mount Diablo, after the winding ascent from the plains, and buy corn on the cob, grilled over coals or boiled in large aluminium pots in water salted and seasoned with hot peppers, thyme and escallion.

Cornmeal (ground dried corn) is also widely used in Jamaica. It is added to flour to make dumplings, or made into cornmeal pudding or pone (p. 150) or a thick, sweetened and spiced porridge called hominy which is probably of North American influence.

## GARDEN EGG

The garden egg (*Solanum melongena*), also known as egg plant, aubergine or melongene, is a native of South Asia. It is not a popular vegetable in Jamaica, though it is often made into a stew with salt cod.

## INDIAN KALE

This vegetable with heart-shaped leaves (*Xanthosoma sagittisolium*) belongs to the same family as the coco. It is indigenous to Central and South America. We use it in pepperpot and other soups, and it can be cooked and eaten in the same way as callaloo.

## IRISH POTATO

The ordinary potato (*Solanum jasminoides*), which comes originally from South America, is known as 'Irish' in Jamaica to distinguish it from the sweet potato.

## OKRA

The okra (*Hibiscus esculentus*), known also as achro, ladies' fingers, bamia and gumbo, is an annual belonging to the Hibiscus family. The tree, which ranges from 4 to 6 feet (1–2 metres) in height, has large roundish or palmate leaves, and bears erect horn-shaped pods 4–6 inches (10–15 cm) long. The young pods are mucilaginous. We use them in soups such as the pepperpot, and in stews.

## PLANTAIN

The plantain, unlike its cousin the banana, cannot be eaten raw even when ripe. When green, it is usually boiled in soups. Turned (i.e. slightly underripe) or ripe (but not soft) plantains are delicious fried (see p. 68). In the days of the sumptuous dinners of the plantations, roasted green plantains, served in a folded table napkin with the cheese course, were '*de rigueur*'. Sweet plantain tarts are very popular in Jamaica, and the recipe can be found on p. 156.

## PUMPKIN

The West Indian pumpkin is a member of the Cucurbitaceae genus, and is also known as green pumpkin or calabaza in Latin America. Although it is similar to the North American pumpkin, it is different in texture and taste. It makes a superb soup, is excellent puréed, and is often served boiled, with butter.

## SUSUMBER

The susumber or gully bean (*Solanum torvum*) is of the same genus as the aubergine or egg plant (and nothing like the cucumber). Once we had a susumber plant grafted with the egg plant, so that it bore both fruits on the same tree. The fruits grow in clusters between the leaf and stem, and are the size of big peas, dark green in colour. They are slightly bitter, and one has to acquire the taste for them. It is best to discard the mature fruit and eat the immature ones. They are usually added to ackee and saltfish and cooked in combination with salted cod.

## SWEET POTATO

The sweet potato (*Ipomoea batatas*) is a trailing perennial producing succulent tuberous roots. It is native to the American tropics, and widely cultivated in warm countries. In the United States of America it is often referred to as yam, but they are not at all related.

Sweet potatoes are delicious baked in charcoals or in the oven. They are also eaten plainly boiled, fried or as potato pudding. When puréed, they are similar in consistency to puréed chestnuts.

## YAMS

Yams, of the Dioscorea genus, are in fact portions of underground stems known as tubers. The aerial portions of yam plants are climbing vines which die after each growing season, while the tubers store up food and other materials to start the growth for the following season.

Originally the greater yams were introduced by the Portuguese from West Africa, where they were known as 'nyam'. The only yams originating in the American tropics are the 'yampie' or Indian yam (*D. trifida*), and the mild yam or bitter Jessie (*D. polygonoide*), found in woodlands and shaded gullies.

Some yams are hard in texture when cooked and some soft. The hard ones are preferable for soups and salads. Yams are boiled and served as an accompaniment to meats, or added to soups. They can be used in the same way as potatoes or other tubers.

Here are a few of the great number of known yams:

*White yam* – a hard-textured yam.
*Yellow yam* – firm, yellow, excellent in soups.
*Negro yam* – soft white yam.
*Lucea yam* – soft white yam, well flavoured, grown in the hills of Hanover. Very popular.
*Renta* – a white yam.
*St Vincent* – a white yam which must be eaten as soon as it is harvested or bought.
*Thaw* – resembles a cross between a negro yam and a yellow yam.
*Yampie* – excellent yam of three varieties, the white, red and purple.
*Chinese yam* – this is a variety of white yam.

All or most of these yams should be available in the U.K.

# ✤ PULSES

Pulses make up a fair percentage of the protein intake of Jamaicans and are used in soups, stews and rice dishes.

The *red pea, French or kidney bean* (*Phaseolus vulgaris*) is the most popular pulse. We use two varieties: a small, mottled local variety, which makes very good rice and peas, and a larger, dark red variety which is starchier and therefore good for soups and stews. Both are generally sold dried, though they are available fresh.

The *gungo pea, congo or pigeon pea* (*Cajanus indicus*) is probably native to the East Indies, and is thought to have been introduced into Jamaica from West Africa by the Spanish. It is available fresh from November to February and dried the rest of the year.

*Butter, broad and Lima beans* are also popular, and are used mainly as an addition to stews such as oxtail and beans, cowfoot and beans and tripe and beans.

*Cow peas and black eye peas* are both varieties of *Vigna linguiculata*. Cow peas are brown with white markings, and black eye peas white with black markings. Both are used in more or less the same way as red peas and gungo peas.

## CURRIED ACKEES

12 ackees in pods
1 onion *or* 3 stalks escallion
1 small tomato
1 fl oz (25 ml) oil
2 tablespoons curry powder (p. 28)

¼ cup (2 fl oz, 50 ml) water
salt
pepper

Clean the ackees, boil them until just tender, then drain. In the meantime, chop the onion or escallion and the tomato. Heat the oil and gently fry the onion or escallion, then add the tomato and curry powder and stir well. Add the water, then the drained ackees, and simmer for 5 minutes. Season with salt and pepper and serve at once.

### ✳PROVERB✳

Ackee lub fat, okra lub salt.

## ACKRA CAKES

2 cups (1 lb, 500 g) black eye peas
hot pepper
salt

pepper
oil for deep frying

Soak the peas in lots of cold water overnight. When you are ready to make the ackras, rub the skin off the peas and pound them in a mortar. Add some hot pepper (as much as you like), then salt and pepper to taste. Beat the mixture until it is very light; pour in a little water if necessary. Heat the oil and drop in spoonfuls of the mixture. They will be done when golden in colour.

Ackra cakes are of West African origin but are very similar to the 'falafel' of Egypt.

## ROAST BREADFRUIT

The most esteemed breadfruit for roasting is the yellow heart. It usually has a firm but moist texture, and is delicious served hot with lots of butter. This variety is not common, however, and in any case I have found it almost impossible to tell the difference between the ordinary breadfruit and the yellow heart one.

Breadfruits, mature but not ripe, are roasted either on a coal stove or on one of the rings of a gas stove, or baked in the oven. In the case of the coalpot or gas stove, all that is necessary is that the breadfruit be turned until the whole fruit is brown. If the breadfruit is to be baked in the oven this should take 30–45 minutes at 350°F, 180°C, gas 4; test it with a skewer or knife to see if it is soft. To peel the hot breadfruit, fold a kitchen cloth in four, rest the breadfruit on it, and peel it while holding it with the other hand. Halve it, remove the centre, and cut it in slices. Arrange on a platter and dot with lumps of butter.

## STUFFED BREADFRUIT WITH ACKEE AND SALTFISH

1 mature breadfruit                    ackee and saltfish (see p. 77)

Roast the breadfruit as in the previous recipe. After peeling it, cut a small piece from the bottom so that it will be able to sit, and cut a 1-inch (3-cm) slice from the top. Using a sharp knife, remove the heart or core and some of the flesh. Fill the breadfruit with the hot ackee and saltfish, then arrange it on a platter, perhaps surrounding it with slices of avocado pear, sprigs of parsley or watercress, and serve while hot. It does make a magnificent dish. Enough for 4.

## BOILED BREADFRUIT

Boiled breadfruit is traditionally served as an accompaniment to meat, fish or poultry. The unripe or green fruit is used. It is peeled,

cut into slices and boiled in salted water like potatoes or green
bananas.

## BREADFRUIT IN COCONUT SAUCE

½ lb (250 g) bacon
3 stalks escallion, chopped
1 tomato, chopped
1 sprig thyme
3 slices hot pepper

2½ cups (1 pint, 600 ml) coconut
milk (see p. 135)
1 immature breadfruit, peeled and
sliced

Place a large frying pan or skillet on a low heat. Add the bacon, cut
in 2-inch (5-cm) strips. When the bacon fat runs, add the escallion,
tomato, thyme and hot pepper. Stir. Add the coconut milk and
bring to the boil. Lower the heat and add salt, pepper and the
breadfruit. Cover and simmer for 30 minutes, or until the breadfruit is tender and the sauce turns oily. Enough for 4–5.

## BAKED CHO CHOS

3 cho chos, halved
¼ teaspoon thyme leaves
¼ teaspoon chopped hot pepper
2 tablespoons (1 oz, 25 g) butter

½ lb (250 g) minced beef or fish
salt
black pepper
1 cup (½ lb, 250 g) grated cheese

Boil the cho chos in lightly salted water until they are tender, then
remove them from the water and drain. Scoop out the pulp,
leaving a little so that the skins are not broken. Mix the pulp with
the thyme, hot pepper, butter, and meat or fish. Add salt and black
pepper to taste. Fill the shells with the mixture. Arrange them on
an oiled baking sheet or in a large oiled ovenproof dish, sprinkle
them with the cheese, and bake in a moderate oven until the tops
are golden – about 30–45 minutes.

# TURN CORNMEAL

| | |
|---|---|
| 1 oz (25 g) salt pork | ½ cup (6 oz, 175 g) shredded raw |
| oil | salt cod |
| 1 medium-sized onion, chopped | 5 cups (2 pints, 1.25 litres) |
| 3 stalks escallion, chopped | coconut milk (see p. 135) |
| 1 tomato, chopped | black pepper |
| 4 slices hot pepper, chopped | 2 cups (12 oz, 350 g) cornmeal |
| 6 okras, chopped | |

Cut the salt pork into small pieces and fry them in a little oil in a wide heavy pan until golden in colour. Set aside. Sauté the onion and escallion in the same pan, adding a little more oil. Throw in the tomato, hot pepper, okras, salt cod and salt pork. Stir for a few minutes, then pour in the coconut milk. Let it come to the boil, add the black pepper, then gradually add the cornmeal, stirring it all the time. Little by little, the cornmeal will swell considerably. Turn the heat to very low, cover the pan, and cook for another 15–20 minutes. It is delicious served as an accompaniment to brown stew fish (p. 82). Enough for 4.

# CALLALOO IN BUTTER

| | |
|---|---|
| 2 lb (1 kg) callaloo | black pepper |
| ½ cup (4 oz, 125 g) butter | ¼ teaspoon grated nutmeg |
| salt | |

Wash the callaloo thoroughly in lots of water, discarding any old leaves and the seeds at the top. Chop into small pieces and boil in a large pan of water until tender. Remove the pan from the heat and drain the callaloo in a sieve. Heat the butter until it begins to sizzle. Add the well drained callaloo and turn it thoroughly in the butter, adding salt and pepper to taste and a few gratings of nutmeg.

This must be served immediately. Indian kale can also be prepared in this way. Enough for 4.

## FRIED PLANTAINS

Remove the skins from the plantains and either cut them crosswise or cut each one in three and then again lengthwise. Fry them in a little oil until golden brown. Drain them on kitchen paper and serve them hot, arranged on a platter.

## BAKED PLANTAINS

Cut the ripe plantains in three crosswise, keeping the skin still attached on one side. Place them on an oiled sheet and bake until puffed and tender.

## BOILED PUMPKIN

Pumpkin is usually eaten boiled. It must be well drained. It is served with butter, and some people like a sprinkling of black pepper.

It can also be served puréed with butter, salt and pepper.

## CANDIED SWEET POTATOES

2 lb (1 kg) sweet potatoes
¼ cup (2 oz, 50 g) butter

¼ teaspoon grated nutmeg
½ cup (¼ pint, 150 ml) water

Boil the sweet potatoes in their skins in some slightly salted water until tender, then drain them and remove the skins. Slice the potatoes and arrange them in layers in a buttered ovenproof dish, each layer dotted with butter and sprinkled with grated nutmeg. Repeat the layers until the dish is full. Add the water, and bake for 45 minutes or until the top is crisp.

Sweet potatoes are also eaten plainly boiled, or puréed as in the previous recipe, when they are similar in taste to puréed chestnuts.

# RICE AND PEAS

Various versions of rice and peas exist in the Caribbean, but none has become such a major part of the national cuisine as the Jamaican one. It is usually an important part of Sunday lunch and festive meals. It was not mentioned in Sullivan's *Jamaica Cookery Book* (1893), but appears to have become popular some time after this date.

| | |
|---|---|
| 1 cup (8 oz, 250 g) red kidney beans | 1 sprig thyme |
| | 3 slices hot pepper |
| 1 mature coconut, grated, *or* 1 packet coconut cream | 1 clove garlic, crushed |
| | 1 stalk escallion, crushed |
| 6 cups (2½ pints, 1.5 litres) water | 2¼ cups (1 lb, 500 g) rice |
| ½ lb (250 g) salt beef *or* pig's tail (optional) | black pepper |
| | salt |

If you are doubtful about the age of your beans, soak them overnight. To make coconut milk, add the water to the grated coconut, mix well, squeeze the coconut with your hands to extract as much milk as possible, and press through a sieve. Alternatively, add the packet of coconut cream to the water.

Clean the beans of any grit and wash them. Put them in a medium-sized pan which has a tight fitting lid. Add the coconut milk and the salt beef or pig's tail. Bring to the boil, then lower the heat and cook until the beans are tender – the time will vary according to their age, but they should be cooked in 1–2 hours if they are dried, less if they are fresh. Add the thyme, hot pepper, garlic, escallion and black pepper, and salt only if this is needed. (The mixture should be quite salty at this stage.) Simmer for a few minutes, then add the rice, which should be washed just before it is added.

The liquid now should be about 1 inch (2.5 cm) above the rice, so add water if necessary. Cover the pot, bring to the boil once again, then immediately turn the heat to low. The rice will be ready as soon as the liquid disappears and each grain of rice is separate. Just before serving, stir to ensure even distribution of the beans. Enough for 6.

Rice and peas made with green gungo peas is prepared in the same way, and heralds the Christmas and New Year season.

# FISH
# AND SHELLFISH

As to fish, Savanna-la-Mar is reckoned the best place in the island, both for variety and SAFETY, for, in many parts, the fish feed upon copperas banks, and cannot be used without much precaution; here, none is necessary, and it is only to be wished that their names equalled their flesh in taste; for it must be owned, that nothing can be less tempting than the sounds of Jew-fish, hog fish, mud fish, snappers, god-dammies, groupas and grunts! Of the sea fish which I have hitherto met with, the deep water silk appears to me the best; and of the rivers, the Mountain mullet; but indeed, the fish is generally so excellent, and in such profusion, that I never sit down to table without wishing for the company of Queen Atygatis of Scythe, who was so particularly fond of fish that she prohibited all her subjects from eating it on pain of death, through fear that there might not be enough left for her majesty.

M. G. Lewis, *Journal of a West Indian Proprietor*, 1834

Some years ago, returning to Kingston from Ocho Rios via Spanish Town, I purchased a string of river mullet from a lone vendor just beyond the Flat Bridge. The fish were still alive when we arrived home. It took me some time to scale the fish, as in my ignorance I kept pouring water over them which only served to revive them. Eventually they became quiet, then they were prepared for the barbecue. First they were rubbed with salt, pepper and lime juice, a little sweet basil and oil were sprinkled over them, and they were left to marinate for half an hour. They were then grilled on charcoal. They were exquisite. We have never had grilled fish since then which could be compared with those mullet. Perhaps it was a combination of the freshness of the fish, the seasonings and the charcoal grilling.

Now each time we return from the North Coast via the Flat Bridge we are on the lookout for a man holding a string of fish. Alas, we have never so far been able to repeat the wonderful experience.

Despite the abundance of fresh fish from our sea, rivers and mountain streams, salted fish has played a very important part in our history since it was imported to feed the slaves. Monk Lewis, in *Journal of a West Indian Proprietor*, noted the fondness which the slaves acquired for salted provisions.

... the slaves also receive from their owners a regular weekly allowance of red herrings and salt meat which serves to relish their vegetable diet; and indeed they are so passionately fond of salted provisions that instead of giving them fresh beef (as at their festival of Saturday last) I have been advised to provide some hogsheads of salt fish, as likely to afford them more gratification, at such future additional holidays I may find possible to allow them in this busy season of crop.

The recipes developed by the slaves, combining this valuable source of protein with various vegetables, have greatly influenced West Indian cooking, and this lowly food has been adopted by the whole community. Indeed, recent shortages made the humble saltfish a luxury item, and one is sometimes tempted to salt fresh fish in order to be able to produce a favourite dish. (Directions for salting fish can be found on p. 223.)

At one time our sea, rivers and streams provided plentiful supplies of crustaceans: lobsters, shrimps, white and the highly esteemed black crabs, and jongas. Now these have become expensive and scarce, possibly owing to the destruction of feeding grounds and the pollution of our waters.

Before the recipes, I include a list of our fish and shellfish.

## ❋PROVERB❋

**Fish a deep water no know how fish a riber-side feel.**

## CALEPEAVER
This is the largest of the mullets, also known as Jamaica salmon, as it tastes similar to that fish. It is an excellent fish but not very commonly known. It used to be plentiful at the mouth of the Rio Cobre river near Spanish Town. The name is of Tupí origin, coming from the Brazilian Portuguese adaptation of it, *carapeba*.

## CONCH
The conch is a large mollusc whose shell is a delicate shade of pink, darkening to a deeper pink towards the inside. The flesh is somewhat rubbery in texture, but it makes an excellent chowder or soup, stew and fritters.

## CRABS
There are both land and sea crabs. The land crabs are black or white,

the former being the tastiest and the most sought after. The white crabs are also very good, the flesh more resembling that of the lobster or crayfish.

## CUTLASS
This is a long thin bony fish, best used for soup.

## GOAT
This is so called because of the beard or whiskers. It is not unlike the mullet in texture, and is good for frying or baking.

## GROUPER
This is a fine fish, good cooked any way. Groupers can be very large.

## JACK
These are of many colours – silver yellow or butter, yellow tail, greenback, burnfin, black and amber jack. They can be as large as 150 lb (68 kg), and are good for eating.

## JONGA, JANGA
The jonga is a crayfish, found under rocks in rivers. Some are shrimp-coloured and some dark, almost black, but all turn red when cooked.

## JUNE FISH, JEW FISH
This is a small fish which tends to be dry and light in texture. It is usually stewed in a rich sauce.

## KINGFISH
This is a large meaty fish, excellent for grilling or pickling, but slightly on the dry side.

## LOBSTER
This is really a crayfish, but it is cooked in the same way as lobster.

## MACKEREL
These are imported pickled.

## MARLIN (BLUE)
This is a large game fish, weighing upwards of 150 lb (68 kg). Marlin steaks are excellent for grilling. It is superb when smoked and thinly sliced like salmon.

## MULLET (MOUNTAIN)
This is a freshwater fish found in rivers. The flavour is superb – this fish has had a reputation as a delicacy for over 200 years. It is best grilled over charcoal, though rarely seen for sale.

### OLD WIFE

This is a small flat fish with a stiff thick skin which must be removed before cooking. The markings around the eyes suggest wrinkles, hence the name. It is usually fried.

### OYSTERS

These are small swamp oysters, gathered from the exposed roots of the mangrove in the swamps. They are usually eaten with a hot pepper sauce.

### PARROT

The parrot is a fish of many beautiful colours. It is a good eating fish, and can be cooked in any way.

### RED HERRING

Herrings are imported smoked. The skin and bones are removed before the fish are made into a pickled salad. They are one of the ingredients for Solomon Gundy.

### SALTFISH

This is the local name for salted imported cod.

### SHAD

These are imported pickled.

### SHRIMPS

These are usually curried or boiled in spiced water. Peppered shrimps are a speciality along the coast road of the parish of St Elizabeth.

### SNAPPER

This is probably the most popular of our fish. It is somewhat like the red mullet but of a finer quality. It comes in many colours – red, black, grey, yellow tail, red tail and red belly.

### SPRATS

These are small fish, somewhat like sardines, though slightly larger. They are usually fried or pickled.

### TURTLE

Turtle used to be plentiful here at one time, but is now almost extinct. It can be made into cutlets and steaks, or used in stews or a delicious soup.

# ACKEE AND SALTFISH

This is Jamaica's national dish and a worthy one, with its beguiling contrast of flavours.

| | |
|---|---|
| 2 dozen ackees in pods | 1 sprig thyme |
| ½ lb (250 g) salt cod | 3–4 slices hot pepper |
| 2 tablespoons (1 oz, 25 g) butter | 1 small tomato, chopped |
| ¼ cup (2 fl oz, 50 ml) oil | (optional) |
| 2 onions, sliced | black pepper |

Choose ackees that are completely open, with the black seed and yellow fruit clearly visible in the scarlet pod. This is important, as unripe ackees contain a highly toxic substance.

Remove the ackees from the pods. Discard the seeds and the pink membrane found in the cleft of each fruit. Wash them and put them to boil in a large pot of water with the salt fish. (My mother used to tie them in a muslin bag and drop the bag into the water with the fish. This prevents the ackees from disintegrating.) As soon as the ackees are tender, pour the contents of the pot into a large sieve, discarding the water. Separate the ackees from the fish. Run some cold water over the fish so that you can remove the bones and skin comfortably, then flake it and set it aside.

Put the butter and oil to heat in a frying pan. Add the onions, thyme and hot pepper slices, and the tomato if desired. Stir for a few minutes then add the flaked fish. Stir for a few more minutes then add the drained ackees, carefully stirring so as not to crush them – this is a matter of taste, as some people do not like the ackees crushed. Add a little more oil if necessary, sprinkle with plenty of freshly ground black pepper, and the dish is ready.

Serve it decorated with halved hard-boiled eggs. If the dish is a main course, avocado pear slices, fried plantains, bammies, yams, dumplings and roasted breadfruit all make fine accompaniments. Serves 4.

Ackee and saltfish also makes a very good starter when served with thin slices of avocado, or as ackee pie: line a pie tin with pastry (see p. 153), fill it with ackee and saltfish, sprinkle with cheese, and bake for 45 minutes at 400°F, 200°C, gas 6. Serve hot.

Try also the ackee and saltfish appetizer on p. 33.

**RIDDLE:** Me fader send me to pick out a wife, tell me to tek only those that smile, fe those that do not smile wi kill me.

**ANSWER:** Ackees

## SALTFISH AND PAWPAW

½ lb (250 g) salt cod
2 lb (1 kg) green pawpaw
6 rashers of bacon
oil
2 onions, chopped

1 tomato, chopped
4 slices hot pepper
1 sprig thyme
1 cup (8 fl oz, 250 ml) water

Boil the salt cod in water for 15 minutes. In the meantime peel and slice the pawpaw, discard the seeds, and set it aside. When the fish is cooked, put it under some running water to cool, then remove the skin and bones and flake the fish.

Fry the bacon in a little oil, then remove from the pan and set aside. Add the onions, tomato, hot pepper and thyme to the pan. Stir for a few minutes then add the flaked fish; stir again and add the sliced pawpaw. Pour in the water, cover the pan, and simmer until the pawpaw is tender and the liquid is reduced to a gravy. Garnish the saltfish and pawpaw with the rashers of bacon, and serve it with boiled yams, bananas or roasted breadfruit. Serves 4.

## SUSUMBER AND SALTFISH

½ lb (250 g) salt cod
2 cups (1 lb, 500 g) young
  susumbers
1 onion *or* 3 stalks escallion,
  sliced

1 tomato, chopped
1 sprig thyme
4 slices hot pepper
¼ cup (2 fl oz, 50 ml) oil

Boil the salt cod and susumbers in a good quantity of water. When the susumbers are tender, pour the contents of the pot into a sieve to drain. Flake the fish and set it aside. Fry the onion, tomato, thyme and hot pepper in the oil, then add the flaked fish. Mix well, stir for a few minutes, then add the susumbers. Cover the pan and allow to simmer for 5 minutes.

Serve it with hard dough bread, boiled yams, bananas, or roasted breadfruit. Serves 3–4.

## SALTFISH SALAD

Variations of this salad exist throughout the Caribbean. In St Lucia it is known as Brule Jol, in Trinidad and Tobago as Buljol.

1 lb (500 g) salt cod
1 cucumber, peeled and sliced
2 tomatoes, cut in wedges
2 tablespoons vinegar *or* lime juice
3 tablespoons salad oil

1 hot pepper, Scotch bonnet if possible, sliced and with seeds removed
black pepper
hard-boiled eggs (optional)
parsley (optional)

Soak the fish in plenty of water for at least 2 hours to remove the excess salt. Then remove the skin and bones and flake the fish. Place it in a bowl and add the cucumber, tomatoes, vinegar or lime juice, oil and hot pepper. Mix well and adjust the seasoning. If you like, garnish the salad with halved hard-boiled eggs and a sprinkling of chopped parsley.

Avocado slices, hard dough bread and roasted breadfruit make ideal accompaniments. This salad is good for a light lunch. Serves 4.

## SALTFISH AND RICE

½ lb (250 g) salt cod
¼ cup (2 fl oz, 50 ml) oil
1 onion, chopped
2 stalks escallion *or* onion, chopped
1 clove garlic, chopped

2 tomatoes, chopped
3 slices hot pepper
1 cup (8 oz, 500 g) cooked susumber (optional)
2 cups (14 oz, 400 g) rice, washed
2 cups (¾ pint, 500 ml) water

Soak the salt cod in water for 30 minutes, then remove the skin and bones and shred the fish. Heat the oil in a frying pan and gently sauté the onion or escallion and garlic. Stir in the shredded fish. Cook for a few minutes then add the tomatoes, hot pepper and susumber and stir again. Now add the rice to the pan, stirring so that everything is well amalgamated and all the rice grains are coated with the oil.

Pour in exactly 2 cups of water, the same quantity as the rice. Stir, cover the pan, bring to the boil, then lower the heat. The rice should be ready in 20 minutes. This is an ideal luncheon dish, served with avocado pear slices, fried plantains and a salad. Enough for 2.

## RUN DOWN

| | |
|---|---|
| 2 coconuts, grated | 3 stalks escallion, chopped |
| 6 cups (2½ pints, 1.5 litres) water | 3 tomatoes, chopped |
| 2 lb (1 kg) pickled mackerel *or* shad | 1 hot pepper, Scotch bonnet if possible, chopped and seeds removed |
| 2 onions, chopped | |
| 1 clove garlic, chopped | 2–3 sprigs thyme |

Add the water to the grated coconut and press the liquid through a sieve or muslin bag. Set this coconut milk aside. Soak the mackerel or shad in water for at least 3 hours to remove excess salt, remove as many bones as possible and set this aside also.

Boil the coconut milk rapidly in a heavy frying pan until it is reduced to something resembling curdled custard and oil. Add the fish, cover, and cook for 10 minutes on a medium heat. Stir in the onion, garlic, escallion, tomatoes, hot pepper and thyme, lower the heat, and simmer for a further 10 minutes.

This dish is traditionally served with boiled green bananas and dumplings. Sometimes the green bananas are cooked with it. Serves 4–5.

# ESCOVEITCH FISH

Escoveitch fish and variations of it are found in many Latin American countries. The dish originated in southern Spain and France, where it appears as '*escabeche*'. Older forms of the word recorded by Cassidy in Jamaica (*Dictionary of Jamaican English*) are 'scaveech' or 'caveach', distortions of the original word. The meaning of the word was 'to pickle', a method of preserving meat and fish which was popular in the days before refrigeration. Fish prepared in this manner would last between 2 and 3 days. Elizabeth David, in *Spices, Salt and Aromatics in the English Kitchen*, notes that catsup was derived from caveach, a form of vinegar pickle in which cooked fish was preserved.

Snapper, jack, sprats, parrot, grunt and kingfish are best for this dish, but any fish will do. The secret of success lies in the freshness of the fish. When you are buying fish make sure that the eyes are bright and shiny and the gills red.

| | |
|---|---|
| 2 lb (1 kg) fresh fish | 2 onions, sliced |
| juice of 2 limes | 2 hot peppers, Scotch bonnet if |
| salt | possible, sliced |
| black pepper | 2 tablespoons pimento berries |
| oil | 1 cup (8 fl oz, 250 ml) vinegar |
| *Pickle* | salt |
| 1–2 cho chos *or* cucumbers | |

Clean and wash the fish, rub them with the lime juice, and dry them with a kitchen cloth or paper. Sprinkle them on both sides and inside with salt and pepper. Heat plenty of oil in a frying pan until it is very hot and begins to smoke very slightly. Place the fish in the hot oil one at a time, taking care that they do not overlap. Reduce the heat a little and fry the fish on both sides. If they are difficult to turn, then the oil was not hot enough. Leave them for a further couple of minutes to allow the underside to brown, then turn. When the fish are done, drain them and arrange them on a large platter or in a deep bowl.

In the meantime, peel the cho chos and cut them into halves and then into long strips. Put them in a saucepan with the onions, hot peppers, pimento, vinegar and a little salt to taste. Bring the mixture to the boil, simmer for 2 minutes or so, then remove it from the heat. Pour this hot pickle over the fish. The fish is often left to marinate in the pickle for a while (it will keep for up to 3 days), but I prefer to serve the dish while the pickle ingredients are still crisp. Serve it hot or cold.

Escoveitch fish is traditionally served with bammies, hard-dough bread or johnny cakes, and fresh lemonade. It is often eaten at Sunday breakfast. Enough for 4–5.

## BROWN STEW FISH

2 lb (1 kg) fresh snapper *or* kingfish (or, failing these, mackerel, cod or red mullet)
juice of 2 limes
oil
2 onions, sliced
1 clove garlic, chopped
2 tomatoes, chopped

3–4 slices hot pepper, Scotch bonnet if possible
1 tablespoon pimento berries
1½–2 cups (12–15 fl oz, 350–450 ml) water
salt
black pepper

Clean and wash the fish, rub them with the lime juice, then dry them with a kitchen cloth or paper. Fry them as described in the previous recipe. Remove some of the oil from the frying pan, leaving just enough to coat the bottom of the pan. Add the onions, garlic, tomatoes, hot pepper slices and pimento berries. Stir for a few minutes, then add the water, salt and black pepper. Bring to the boil, then reduce the heat, cover the pan and simmer for 10 minutes until the sauce is reduced.

Brown stew fish is delicious served with turn cornmeal. Enough for 4.

## ✱ CRABS

My brothers and their friends would cycle from Spanish Town to Port Henderson at night to catch crabs during the crabbing season, usually after heavy rains, when the crabs would be flooded out of their holes. In those days the area was a very peaceful bay with swamps, mangroves, mosquitoes and sandflies! My brothers would return in the early hours of the morning, their cycles laden with sacks of white crabs. These were thrown into a large cistern in the yard which was then covered so that the crabs could not escape.

The next day the entire household buzzed with activity, for the crabs had to be boiled in large containers either on wood or on a coalpot. As we picked the meat from the boiled crabs, we ate, but the bulk of the crab meat was destined for supper in the form of baked crabs in their backs, or curried crab.

The more highly esteemed black crabs were to be found only in certain areas of the island. Once a year, it is said, they march down from the hills, where they live in cracks and crevices, to the seaside to spawn and to change their shells. Nothing short of a river diverts them. I have been told that during this rush to the seaside, they can be heard at night crawling over houses. This is the time when they are caught, and the female crabs laden with eggs are the prize catches. Alas, the black crabs are no longer as numerous as they used to be.

### ❋PROVERB❋

**When crab walk too much him los' him claw.**

## BOILED CRABS

The crabs are usually kept on a diet of greens for a few days to clean them out before they are eaten.

Put a large pot of water on to boil. Drop in a few slices of hot pepper, some chopped escallion, a few sprigs of thyme and some salt. Pick up the live crabs and drop them into the boiling water, one at a time, until the pot is full, but make sure there is enough water to cover them. Boil for about 30 minutes.

The picking of the crab meat from the shells is a tedious business, made more enjoyable by the company of others. Break off the claws, break the shells and remove as much of the meat as possible. Remove the back of the crab, discard the water and black matter, and search for the salmon-coloured eggs in the back if they are females – place these with the picked meat. Break the shell of the remaining bits and remove the meat.

You can, of course, serve the crabs straight from the pot, and eat the meat as you remove it from the shells.

## BAKED CRABS

| | |
|---|---|
| 2 dozen boiled crabs | ¼ teaspoon thyme leaves |
| 1 onion | 4 tablespoons (2 oz, 50 g) butter |
| 2 stalks escallion *or* spring onion | breadcrumbs |
| 4–5 slices hot pepper, seeds removed | salt |
| | black pepper |

Remove the meat from the crabs as described in the previous recipe, keeping the backs. Prepare the seasonings by grating the onion and chopping the escallion and the hot pepper finely. Add these with the thyme leaves to the crab meat. Mix in the butter and some breadcrumbs – just enough to hold the meat together. Add pepper and salt to taste.

Wash and dry the crab backs and fill them with the seasoned meat. Cover each with a sprinkling of breadcrumbs and a few dots of butter and bake at 350°F, 180°C, gas 4, until brown. Enough for 6.

## CURRIED CRAB

| | |
|---|---|
| 1 fl oz (25 ml) oil | 3–4 slices hot pepper, chopped |
| 2 tablespoons (1 oz, 25 g) butter | 1½ cups (12 fl oz, 350 ml) water |
| 1 large onion, chopped | 2 cups (approx. 1 lb, 500 g) |
| 1 clove garlic, chopped | cooked crab meat (about 12 |
| 2 tablespoons curry powder (see p. 28) | crabs) |
| 2 tomatoes, chopped | salt |
| 2 sweet peppers, sliced | pepper |

In a deep frying pan, heat the oil and butter until they start to sizzle. Add the onion and garlic, stir for a few minutes, then add the curry powder. Throw in the tomatoes, sweet peppers and hot pepper. Stir again, then add the water, bring to the boil, lower the heat and throw in the crab meat. Add salt and pepper. Simmer for 10 minutes, until the liquid is reduced to the desired thickness. Enough for 4.

Serve with rice, fried plantains, avocado slices, mango chutney, grated coconut (the dark outer layer having been removed) and a salad.

## CURRIED LOBSTER

1 fl oz (25 ml) oil
2 tablespoons (1 oz, 25 g) butter
2 onions, chopped
1 clove garlic, chopped
2 tablespoons curry powder (see p. 28)
2 tomatoes, chopped

2 sweet peppers, sliced
4 slices hot pepper, chopped
3 cups (1¼ pints, 750 ml) water
2 lb (1 kg) boiled lobster meat
salt
black pepper

Prepare in the same way as curried crab, above. These quantities should be enough for 5–6.

## CURRIED SHRIMPS

2 lb (1 kg) fresh shrimps
2 tablespoons (1 oz, 25 g) butter
1 fl oz (25 ml) oil
2 onions, chopped
2 cloves garlic, chopped
2 tablespoons curry powder (see p. 28)

1 tomato, chopped
3–4 slices hot pepper
1 sweet pepper, chopped (optional)
salt
black pepper
1½ cups (12 fl oz, 350 ml) water

Shell the shrimps, then fry them gently in the butter and oil with the onions and garlic. Add the curry powder, stirring it in for a few seconds, then add the tomato, hot pepper, sweet pepper, salt and pepper. Pour in the water, bring to the boil, then lower the heat to medium. The dish should be ready in 10 minutes or when the sauce has reduced and thickened. (On no account add any thickening.) Serve with rice. Enough for 4.

## SHRIMP AND RICE

2 rashers bacon, diced
1 fl oz (25 ml) oil
1 onion, chopped
1 clove garlic, chopped
2 lb (1 kg) fresh shrimps, shelled
2 tomatoes, chopped
1 sweet pepper, diced

3 slices hot pepper, chopped
¼ teaspoon thyme leaves
salt
black pepper
2 cups (14 oz, 400 g) rice, washed
2 cups (¾ pint, 450 ml) water

Dice the bacon and fry the pieces in their own fat until they are translucent but not dry. Add the oil and throw in the onion, garlic and raw shrimps. Stir well until the shrimps are pink, then add the tomatoes, sweet and hot peppers, thyme, salt and pepper. Stir well to make sure that all the ingredients are well coated with the fat. Add the rice, then pour in the water. Stir again, bring to the boil, then lower the heat. It should be ready in 20 minutes, by which time the grains of rice should be separate.

This dish goes well with avocado slices and a green salad. Enough for 4.

## TURTLE BALLS

2 lb (1 kg) turtle meat
juice of 1 lime
4 rashers bacon
1 large onion, grated
4 slices hot pepper, chopped
1 teaspoon freshly ground
   pimento

1 egg, beaten
black pepper
salt
breadcrumbs
oil

*Sauce*
1 onion, sliced
2 tomatoes, chopped
3–4 slices hot pepper

2 cups (¾ pint, 500 ml) water
1 teaspoon lime juice
salt
black pepper

Rub the turtle meat with the lime juice and put it through a mincer with the bacon. Add the onion, hot pepper, pimento, beaten egg, black pepper, and salt to taste. Mix the ingredients well with your fingers, adding just enough breadcrumbs to bind the mixture together. Form into little balls and brown them in a little oil in a frying pan. Remove them from the pan and set them aside while you prepare the sauce.

Pour off some of the oil from the frying pan, and throw in the onion, tomatoes and hot pepper. Stir for a few moments, then add the water, lime juice, salt and black pepper to taste, and bring to the boil. Place the turtle balls in the sauce and cook over a medium heat for about 5 minutes. The sauce should have a nice thick consistency. If the sauce is not thickening enough, increase the heat and reduce the liquid. Enough for 4.

### ❋PROVERB❋

When morass ketch fire,
land-turtle look fe mangrove tree.
(Any port in a storm.)

# BEEF, PORK AND
## GOAT

Many of our domesticated animals – cattle, pigs, goats, fowls – were introduced into Jamaica by the Spaniards between 1503 and 1519, usually via Hispaniola, one of the main Spanish strongholds. The animals multiplied quickly and were soon so numerous that they were roaming wild in the countryside. In 1644 Alonso de Espinosa Centeno, a priest and native of the island, wrote to the King of Spain:

The quantity of wild hogs is so great that the inhabitants who go to the mountains every year to make lard to trade in it with Cartagena [Cuba] and other neighbouring lands, with such profit to themselves, leave the meat to spoil. They do the same with the wild cattle using only the hides and fat.

It is interesting to note that the buccaneers of the same period, who were to play an important part in the history of Jamaica, were so called because initially they too hunted wild hogs and cattle on Hispaniola and preserved their meat on 'boucans', the French version of the Indian name for wooden grills, from which came '*boucaniers*' and the English 'buccaneer'. The hunters then sold this preserved meat to passing ships.

When the English ousted the Spaniards from the island in 1655, they found it overrun with wild livestock. The remains of the Spanish livestock farms became known as 'penns', a term which remained in use until fairly recently and still occurs in some place names, such as May Pen. These penns were owned by the white creole population and produced meat to feed the free whites on the island. The slaves were given salted meat and fish to supplement the crops they grew for themselves, and indeed the Europeans went to some lengths to stop the slaves acquiring a taste for fresh meat, sometimes burying dead cattle rather than let the negroes eat the meat. Slaves were not allowed to rear or sell livestock until about 1735, but by the time of emancipation, 100 years or so later, they had a virtual monopoly in the internal market system and the entire population depended on them for supplies of meat, as for most other commodities. One can assume that once they were allowed to rear livestock their diet began to include more meat.

Before the 1950s, meat was sold mainly at the Saturday markets, and of course in the days before refrigeration it had to be eaten within a day or two. Since then, however, the supermarkets and specialist meat shops have taken over as the chief source of meat.

Beef has always been the most popular and most commonly used meat in Jamaica. Caroline Sullivan noted in her *Jamaica Cookery Book* (1893) that:

There will be some surprise and perhaps discomfort on the part of the new-comer who finds that beef of all cuts, is sold at the same price, 6d per lb no matter what you order, unless you arrange with your butcher to give you beef without bone at 7½d per lb . . . But the butchers charge 6d per lb for bone as well as meat, and sometimes one is disappointed to find that when the 'meat' is delivered, one half of it is 'weigh-meat' or large pieces of bone.

The practice of selling all cuts at the same price was widespread until fairly recently, and I am told that it still persists in certain country parts of the island.

According to Sullivan, goat was not a popular meat. She records several recipes for 'kid or goat mutton', but notes the prejudice displayed by many against this meat. She says:

I have heard people say over and over again that no matter *how* disguised 'goat mutton' may be, they would never eat it. Yet these very people have enjoyed it in my presence, so much so in fact as to ask for another helping.

Today, apart from curried goat, there are hardly any recipes for this meat in Jamaica, though the French Antilles seem to have developed several excellent ways of cooking 'le chabris'.

Mutton has never been common in Jamaica. Sullivan gives the price as 1s. per pound, double that of beef, and points out that much of the so-called mutton for sale was in fact goat. There is not much locally produced mutton these days, though some is imported frozen.

Pork is the other main meat in Jamaica and is widely eaten. The Rastafarians, however, do not eat pork.

My favourite dishes are those that have been cooked slowly, producing meat which is so tender that it hardly needs a knife to cut it. Many of our dishes need to be cooked slowly – oxtail, stew peas and so on. Attempts to hurry the process by fast boiling or by the use of a pressure cooker will not produce the same texture and flavour.

Finally, when you have produced a splendid dish, give some thought to its presentation. Simple but imaginative touches can add a great deal, whether they consist of a sprinkling of parsley or chopped escallion, or an attractive dish in which to serve the food.

## ✳PROVERB✳

Buy beef you buy bone, buy lan' you buy rock-a-tone.

## BEEF AND OKRA

This dish is reminiscent of the Middle Eastern dish 'bamia'. I have often found a parallel between Middle Eastern dishes and our own, especially the slowly cooked meats that can almost be eaten with a spoon, though the spicing is quite different.

| | |
|---|---|
| 2 lb (1 kg) shoulder steak, round of beef, sirloin *or* shin of beef | 1 clove garlic, chopped |
| salt | 1 sprig thyme |
| black pepper | 2 tomatoes, chopped |
| ⅓ cup (3 fl oz, 75 ml) oil | 4 cups (1½ pints, 1 litre) water |
| 2 onions, chopped | 1 lb (500 g) okras, tops removed |

Cut the meat across the grain into thin slices, no more than 2 × 3 inches (5 × 7 cm), and season them with a little salt and pepper.

Brown the meat in the oil (or a mixture of oil and butter), then add the onions and garlic and stir until these take colour. Add the thyme and tomatoes, stir again, and add the water. Bring to the boil, then lower the heat, cover, and simmer until the meat is tender (about 1 hour for sirloin, longer for other cuts). Add more water if it becomes necessary.

Add the okras, taste for salt, cover, and cook for a further 30 minutes. Enough for 4–5.

This dish is particularly good reheated, as the meat absorbs the aroma of the seasonings, so it can be prepared a day in advance.

## BEEF PATTIES

The French émigrés from Haiti who arrived during the eighteenth century are said to have brought with them the recipe for what has become a national favourite – patties. For a long time these have been the midday meal for many Jamaicans. Patties have a very short life and are at their best eaten straight from the oven. I can assure you that after eating these, you will not be tempted to buy the commercially baked product.

*Pastry*
4 cups (1¼ lb, 600 g) flour
1 tablespoon curry powder (see p. 28) *or* turmeric

1 teaspoon salt
1 cup (8 oz, 250 g) shortening *or* margarine
iced water

Sieve together the flour, curry powder and salt. Work in the shortening or margarine, adding enough iced water to hold the dough together. Wrap it in foil and refrigerate for 12 hours or overnight. Remove the dough 15 minutes before it is to be used. Pull off just enough to make one patty at a time. Roll each piece out and cut into circles approximately 4 inches (10 cm) across (use a saucer for measurement). Sprinkle some flour on each and stack, keeping them fresh by covering them with a damp cloth.

*Filling*
2 onions
3 stalks escallion
2 hot peppers, Scotch bonnets if possible, seeds removed
2 lb (1 kg) minced beef
⅓ cup (3 fl oz, 75 ml) oil

1 lb (500 g) breadcrumbs
1 teaspoon thyme leaves
2 tablespoons curry powder (see p. 28)
salt
black pepper
1 cup (8 fl oz, 250 ml) water

Put the onions, escallion and hot peppers through a mincer or chop very finely by hand. Add to the beef and mix very well. Heat the oil in a frying pan, throw in the meat mixture and stir for about 10 minutes, then add the breadcrumbs, thyme and curry powder, and salt and pepper to taste. Mix well, then add the water. Cover and simmer the mixture for 30 minutes. It should be moist, neither runny nor dry. Leave to cool.

Place enough filling on each circle of pastry to cover half of it, fold the other half over, and seal the edges by crimping them with a fork. Bake the patties on ungreased baking sheets in a preheated oven at 400°F, 200°C, gas 6 for 30–35 minutes or until golden brown. Makes approximately 24.

## OXTAIL AND BEANS

2 lb (1 kg) oxtail, jointed
¼ cup (2 fl oz, 50 ml) oil
5 cups (2 pints, 1.25 litres) water
2 tomatoes, chopped
2 onions, chopped

1 clove garlic, chopped
1 sprig thyme
3 slices hot pepper
salt and black pepper
½ lb (250 g) cooked broad beans

Wash and dry the pieces of oxtail and brown them in the oil. Add 4 cups (1½ pints, 1 litre) of water, bring to the boil, then lower the heat and simmer until the oxtail is tender, adding more water if necessary. Reduce the sauce to a thick gravy by increasing the heat, then add the tomatoes, onions, garlic, thyme, hot pepper, salt and black pepper. Stir for a few minutes, then add the remaining water and the broad beans. Mix them in, lower the heat, cover again, and simmer for 10 minutes or until the water evaporates leaving a thick gravy. Serve with rice. Enough for 4.

Another way of preparing the oxtail is to boil it until tender, and then add the seasonings. Excess liquid is removed by rapid boiling. This second method of preparation gives a less thick, rich sauce, but is perhaps less fattening.

## STEW PEAS AND RICE

½ lb (250 g) pig's tail
½ lb (250 g) salt beef
2 cups (1 lb, 500 g) red peas
2 lb (1 kg) shin of beef
water
1 sprig thyme
1 clove garlic, crushed

2 stalks escallion, crushed
4 slices hot pepper, chopped
1 whole hot pepper (optional)
black pepper
salt
1½ cups (½ lb, 250 g) flour for
   spinners (see method)

Soak the pig's tail and the salt beef in plenty of cold water for an hour. In the meantime, clean the red peas of all grit and fluff, and wash in cold water. Wash the shin of beef and cut into small pieces. Put the peas into a large pan and add the soaked salt beef and pig's tail and the shin of beef. Add enough water to cover the meat and peas completely. Bring to the boil, then lower the heat to medium and simmer until the meat is tender and the peas almost disintegrating. This will take approximately 2 hours. Add water if necessary during the cooking.

When the meat and peas are tender, add the thyme, garlic, escallion, chopped and whole hot pepper and some black pepper. There should be no need for salt, but taste and see.

To make the spinners (tiny dumplings), add to the flour a pinch of salt and enough water to make a smooth dough. Make tiny elongated dumplings by rolling small pieces of dough between the palms. Add these to the stew and they will help to thicken and give body to it. If it is still not thick enough, mash some of the peas against the side of the pot and reduce the liquid by further boiling – not too much, or the peas will stick to the bottom and burn.

Stew peas must be served very hot, as the dish tends to congeal as it gets cold. Serve it with fluffy rice, fried plantains, avocado slices and a salad. Enough for 5–6.

## GUNGO PEAS STEW

3 cups (1½ lb, 750 g) gungo peas  
¼ cup (2 fl oz, 50 ml) oil  
1 clove garlic, chopped  
1 onion, chopped  
2 stalks escallion, chopped  
1 lb (500 g) minced beef  
3 tablespoons curry powder (see p. 28) or turmeric  

2 tomatoes, chopped  
4 slices hot pepper, chopped  
1 sprig thyme  
salt  
black pepper  
2 cups (¾ pint, 500 ml) water  
flour for spinners (see previous recipe)  

Put the gungo peas in a pan with plenty of water, boil until tender, and drain. Heat the oil, throw in the garlic, onion and escallion and stir for a few minutes, then add the minced beef. Stir and brown the meat, then mix in the curry powder, tomatoes, chopped hot pepper and thyme. Add salt and pepper to taste, stir for a few minutes, then mix in the boiled gungo peas and the water.

Bring to the boil, then lower the heat and simmer until the stew thickens. Add a few spinners or dumplings.

Serve with fluffy white rice, avocado slices, fried plantain or whatever else you wish. Enough for 4.

## ROAST BEEF

4 slices hot pepper, chopped
1 large tomato
2 cloves garlic, chopped
1 tablespoon salt
1 tablespoon black pepper
½ teaspoon thyme leaves
5 lb (2.25 kg) sirloin roast
⅓ cup (3 fl oz, 75 ml) oil
1 cup (8 fl oz, 250 ml) water

*Gravy*
2 large onions, sliced
2 tomatoes, chopped
1 clove garlic, chopped
3 slices hot pepper, chopped
salt

Mix together the first six ingredients. Make incisions all over the beef, and put a little of the mixture in each incision, leaving some to rub all over the roast. Tie it with string, place it in a deep bowl, and leave for at least 2 hours, or preferably overnight in the refrigerator.

The beef can be either pot-roasted or cooked in the oven in the usual way. If it is to be pot-roasted, then heat the oil in a heavy iron pot or some other heavy braising pot. Remove the beef from the bowl and brown it all over, then add the water to the remains of the seasonings in the bowl and add this to the browned meat. Lower the heat, cover, and simmer until the meat is tender. This should take about 2 hours. Add the gravy ingredients and any vegetables you wish. Stir for a few minutes and taste for salt. If necessary, add a little water, bring back to simmering point, and serve.

If the meat is to be oven-roasted then transfer the meat from the bowl to a roasting pan. If you like the meat red inside, roast at 500°F, 260°C, gas 10 for about 30 minutes, until brown. If you like well done meat, roast at 400°F, 200°C, gas 6 for about an hour until brown. Remove the meat from the roasting pan and keep warm. Scrape all the drippings into a small saucepan over medium heat, and as soon as they start to sizzle, add the gravy ingredients. Stir for a minute or two, then add 2 cups (¾ pint, 500 ml) of water and bring to the boil. Lower the heat slightly, allow the gravy to reduce to the desired consistency, and add salt to taste. Enough for 8.

Traditionally, roast beef is served with rice and peas, roast breadfruit, yams, sweet potatoes, avocado slices, fried plantains and so on. It is reserved for Sundays and festive occasions.

## TRIPE AND BEANS

2 lb (1 kg) tripe
2 onions, chopped
2 stalks escallion, chopped
1 clove garlic, chopped
1 sprig thyme
2 tablespoons curry powder (see p. 28)

2 tomatoes, chopped
4 slices hot pepper, chopped
salt
black pepper
1 lb (500 g) cooked broad beans

Wash the tripe carefully in plenty of cold water. Cut it into small pieces and put them in a saucepan with water to cover. Bring to the boil, then lower the heat and simmer for 2 hours or until the tripe is tender. Add the onions, escallion, garlic, thyme, curry powder, tomatoes and hot pepper. Add salt and pepper, and a little more water if necessary. Simmer for 5 minutes, then add the cooked broad beans and simmer for a further 5–10 minutes until the liquid is reduced to a thick gravy. Enough for 4.

## COWFOOT AND BEANS

1 whole cow's foot
2 onions, chopped
2 cloves garlic, chopped
2 tomatoes, chopped
2 stalks escallion, chopped
1 sprig thyme

3 slices hot pepper
3 tablespoons curry powder (see p. 28)
salt
black pepper
½ lb (250 g) cooked broad beans

Have the cow's foot cut into small pieces, making sure beforehand that all the hairs have been singed off. Wash and dry the pieces carefully, put them in a large heavy saucepan and cover with plenty of water. Bring to the boil, then lower the heat and simmer until the cow's foot is tender – this should take between 2½ and 3 hours.

Remove the bones and discard. Also remove most of the liquid and reserve (this liquid will make the delicious jelly described on p. 144). Leave just sufficient liquid to make a gravy. Put the saucepan back on the heat and add the onions, garlic, tomatoes, escallion, thyme, hot pepper, curry powder, salt and pepper. Cover the pot and simmer for 10 minutes until the gravy begins to thicken, then add the cooked broad beans and simmer for a further 10 minutes. Taste for salt. Enough for 4.

If you are using dried broad beans, soak them overnight, or for several hours, before attempting to boil them. Cook them gently in water until they are tender – this should take about 2 hours.

Serve this delicious dish with fluffy rice, plantains, avocado slices and a salad.


## JERKED PORK

We had at dinner a land tortoise and a barbecued pig, two of the best and richest dishes that I ever tasted, the latter in particular, which was dressed in the true Maroon fashion being placed on a barbecue, through whose interstices the steam can ascend, filled with peppers and spices of the highest flavour, wrapped in plantain leaves and then buried in a hole filled with hot stones by whose vapour it is baked, no particle of juice being thus suffered to evaporate. I have eaten several other good dishes, but none so excellent as this.

M. G. Lewis, *Journal of a West Indian Proprietor*, 1834

To Jamaican lovers of fine food, jerked pork is very special. 'Jerk' is, according to Cassidy, the English form of a Spanish word of Indian origin, meaning to prepare pork in the manner of the Quichua Indians (of South America). The method of cooking was probably learned from the Indians (if not from the Arawaks who inhabited Jamaica, then from others in the Caribbean), and was preserved by the Maroons, who were the former slaves of the Spanish, reinforced by runaway slaves of the English period. They kept the method secret, but by the nineteenth century the dish had become widely popular at festive dinners and was described by writers such as Trollope and Lady Nugent. The method given above by Lewis is a variation on the normal one.

Zora Neale Hurston, an American anthropologist, actually accompanied the Accompong Maroons on one of their hunting expeditions to the Cockpit country,* where the hogs roamed wild. After a most perilous hunt, a huge boar was killed, but not before it had its revenge, killing a few dogs and injuring one of the men. Here is her description of how the boar was jerked.

They shook each other's hand most solemnly across the body of the hog and kissed each other for dangers past. All this was done with the utmost gravity. Finally Colonel Rowe (then head of the Maroons) said: 'Well, we got him. We have luck!'

Then all of the men began to cut dry wood for a big fire. When the fire began to be lively they cut green bush of a certain kind. They put the pig into the fire on his side and covered him with green bush to sweat him so that they could scrape off the hair. When one side was thoroughly cleaned, they scraped the other side, and then washed the whole to a snowy white and gutted the hog. Everything was now done in high good humour. No effort was made to save the chitterlings and haslets which were referred to as 'the fifth quarter', because there was no way to handle it on the march. All of the bones were removed, seasoned and dried over the fire to cook. It was such a big hog that it took nearly all night to finish cooking. It required two men to turn it over when necessary. While it was being cooked and giving off delicious odours, the men talked and told stories and sang songs. One told the story of Paul Bogle, the Jamaican hero of the war of 1797, who made such a noble fight against the British. Unable to stop the fighting until they could capture the leader, they finally appealed to their new allies, the Maroons, who (some say) betrayed Bogle into the hands of the English. Paul Bogle never knew how it was that he was surprised by the English in a cave and taken. He was hanged with his whole family and the war stopped.

Towards morning we ate our fill of jerked pork. It is more delicious than our American barbecue. It is hard to imagine anything better than

---

* Rugged, hilly territory in the interior to the west of the island, inhabited to this day by descendants of the Maroons.

pork the way the Maroons jerk it. When we had eaten all that we could hold, the rest was packed up with the bones and we started the long trek back to Accompong. My blistered feet told me time and time again that we would never get there, but we finally did. What was left of the wild pig was given to the families and friends of the hunters.

They never sell it because they say they hunt for fun. We came marching in singing the Karamante' songs.

> Blue Yerry, ai!
> Blue Yerri
> Blue Yerry Gallo,
> Blue Yerry.

Our connoisseurs insist that the best jerked pork comes from the parish of Portland – like the Cockpit country, a former Maroon stronghold. Indeed, for years Boston Bay was the only spot I knew of where jerked pork could be bought. There were one or two sheds from which billows of smoke and a delicious aroma emerged, and if one took a closer look one could see the pork being jerked on a high latticed frame over charcoals. The meat was dark, almost black. It was sold by the pound with or without the sausage. Today the jerking of pork is a common sight throughout the island, and there are many roadside stalls where one can buy the meat. Chicken and fish are also prepared in the same way now and sold to passers-by. If you feel enterprising enough to make your own, here is a recipe for jerking a whole pig, followed by a more modest version. The spicing of the meat is extremely important, for it is this and the smoking that give the meat its unique flavour.

## TO JERK A WHOLE PIG

When the pig is killed, the blood is collected and added to the seasonings, which consist of hot pepper, pimento, nutmeg, cinnamon leaves, escallion, salt and pepper. The animal is scraped of all its hair, the entrails are removed, and the meat is washed, dried and, if wished, boned. Then the flesh is rubbed with the seasonings mentioned above.

The pig is placed over a grill or '*pata*' made from green pimento or other sticks standing about one foot above the ground, under which a slow fire is kept burning until the pig is cooked. The meat takes on a very dark colour, almost black, owing to a combination of the blood, the pimento and the smoke from the green sticks and charcoal.

The sausage, a great delicacy, is made from the meat obtained from the boiled head of the pig, seasoned with black pepper, salt, escallion and hot pepper. This seasoned meat is stuffed into the cleaned intestines of the pig and tied at intervals. It is also jerked on the *pata*.

## JERKED PORK CHOPS

4 lb (2 kg) pork chops *or* any other cut
2 oz (50 g) pimento berries
6 stalks escallion, chopped
2–3 hot peppers, chopped, with or without seeds
4 fresh cinnamon leaves, chopped (*or* bay if cinnamon is not available)
salt
black pepper

Wash and dry the pork. Heat the pimento berries in a small frying pan, stirring them for 5 minutes, then put them in a mortar and pound them until they are powdery. Add the escallion, hot peppers, cinnamon or bay leaves, salt and pepper. Pound these together until you have a thick paste. Rub the paste all over the pork and leave it for at least 1 hour or overnight in the refrigerator.

When you are ready to cook, place the seasoned meat on the grill of a barbecue or coalpot. Lift the grill to the highest notch on the barbecue and gently cook the meat over charcoal made from burning green pimento wood. Alternatively use normal charcoal and from time to time throw in some green pimento leaves or sticks. This will give the meat the required aroma. (If you are trying this recipe abroad, try throwing pimento berries on to the charcoal or use aromatic herbs. Bay should be the closest to pimento.) Turn the meat over when one side is done. The pork should be ready in an hour. Serves 4–5.

# ROAST SUCKLING PIG

Wash and dry a 10 lb (5 kg) suckling pig. Rub it inside and out with salt and pepper, and brush the outside with some oil.

Boil some yams or potatoes, mash, and season with chopped onion, escallion, hot pepper, salt and black pepper. Add a little butter and mix it in well. Stuff the pig with this mixture, sew it up and tie the front legs together. Do the same with the back legs. Put a potato in the pig's mouth.

Place the pig on a rack in a baking pan so that the skin will remain crisp, and roast it in a preheated oven at 350°F, 180°C, gas 4, allowing roughly 15 minutes to the pound (½ kg), or 2–2½ hours. Turn it over at half-time and baste it from time to time with its own juice. If the pig is too large for your oven, cut it into two pieces.

When the pig is done, transfer it to a large serving dish and keep it warm while you make a gravy from the juices in the pan. Skim off any excess fat and pour the rest into a saucepan, adding 2 chopped tomatoes, 2 chopped onions, a sprig of thyme, 1–2 cups (½–¾ pint, ¼–½ litre) of water, and salt and pepper to taste. Boil quickly until it reduces and serve it separately.

Serve this splendid dish with a sweet potato purée, fried plantains, avocado slices, rice and peas and whatever else you like. It is of course a dish for a large gathering of people.

### ✱PROVERB✱

Pig ax him mumma say, wha' mek him mout long so; him say – ah, no mine mi pickney; dat someting mek fe me long so, wi mek fi yu long so too. (The young are always surprised at the deformities of the ageing, but as they age they will also experience them.)

# GOAT

One of the best places to be in all the world is St Mary's parish, Jamaica. And the best spot in St Mary's is Port Maria, though all of St Mary's is fine. Old Maker put himself to a lot of trouble to make that part of the island of Jamaica, for everything there is perfect. The sea is the one true celestial blue, and the shore, the promontories, the rocks, and the grass are the models for the rest of the world to take pattern after. If Jamaica is the first island of the West Indies in culture, then St Mary's is the first parish of Jamaica. The people there are alert, keen, well read, and hospitable.

They did something for me there that has never been done for another woman. They gave me a curry goat feed. That is something utterly masculine in every detail. Even a man takes the part of a woman in the 'shay shay' singing and dancing that goes on after the feed.

The curry goat feed was being given at the host's bachelor quarters, on a hill overlooking his banana plantation. It was after sundown when we arrived. Already some of the others were there before us. Around a fire under a clump of mango trees, two or three Hindoos were preparing the food. Our host was setting out several dozen quarts of the famous TTL rum, considered the best in Jamaica. They told me that a feed without TTL was just nothing at all. It must be served or it is no proper curry goat feed.

It appears that there must be a presiding officer at a curry goat feed. He sat at the head of the table and directed the fun. There was a story-telling contest, bits of song, reminiscences that were humorous pokes and gibes at each other. All of this came along with the cock soup. This feast is so masculine that chicken soup would not be allowed. It must be soup from roosters. After the cock soup comes ram goat and rice. No nanny goat in this meal either. It is ram goat or nothing. The third spread was banana dumplings with dip and flash. That is, you dip your boiled banana in the suruwa sauce, flash off the surplus and take a bite.

The band played those famous Jamaican airs, Ten pound ten, Donkey want water, Salaam, and Sally Brown. All strong and raw but magnificent music and dancing. It is to be remembered that curry goat is strong feed, so they could not have feminine music.

Zora Neale Hurston,
*Voodoo Gods*, 1939

We do not know a great deal about the origins of curry goat, but we may assume that the East Indians who came to the island as indentured workers from 1842 onwards first used this method to produce a delicious dish out of what was considered by some a rather inferior meat. Although writers such as Caroline Sullivan (*Jamaica Cookery Book*, 1893) give recipes for goat (including a mild curry using leftover roasted kid), we see no mention of the fiery dish loved by the poorer Jamaicans, even as late as the *Peter Pan Book of Recipes* which was produced in 1929.

As the quotation shows, the curry goat feed seems, at least by 1939, to have developed into a ritual akin to today's bachelor party or stag night before a wedding. Today curry goat has become one of our national dishes, served on festive occasions.

#### *PROVERB*

Goat in a too much grass him bawl,
you tek him put a kitchin corner him climb pon stone.
(One is never satisfied with what one has.)

## CURRY GOAT

2 lb (1 kg) goat meat
salt
black pepper
3 tablespoons curry powder (see p. 28)
1 clove garlic, crushed
2 tomatoes, chopped
2 onions, sliced
2 stalks escallion, chopped
1–2 hot peppers, chopped, with or without seeds
2 tablespoons (1 oz, 25 g) butter
¼ cup (2 fl oz, 50 ml) oil
about 3 cups (1¼ pints, 750 ml) water

Cut the goat meat into small pieces, place them in a bowl, and season with the salt, black pepper, curry powder, garlic, tomatoes, onions, escaliion and hot peppers (remove the seeds from the peppers if you do not want the curry to be too hot). Allow the meat to marinate for at least 30 minutes.

When you are ready to proceed, separate the seasonings from the meat and fry the meat in the butter and oil until it is lightly browned. Add enough water to cover the meat and bring to the boil. Reduce the heat, cover the pan, and simmer until the meat is tender, adding more water if necessary. Stir in the seasonings in which the meat was marinated, taste, cover the pan again, and allow it to simmer for a further 10 minutes or until the seasonings are absorbed into the juice, which should now have more body without being too thick. The dish should not be at all dry.

Some cooks prefer either to boil the meat first then add the seasonings when the meat is tender, or to boil the meat and seasonings together from the start. The choice is yours. Serve this splendid dish with white rice, mango chutney, grated coconut, fried plantains, boiled green bananas or whatever else you like.

# POULTRY

A great many of the provisions for the household can be bought at the door. The back gate bell rings frequently during the morning hours. First comer perhaps is the fruit-woman, with her wooden tray on her head.

Then comes my poultry-woman – quite a character in her way. She is very ready with religious phrases, and says she will bring me some fowls next week, 'please God'. She carries on her head a large, shallow basket, in which sit two or three couples of disconsolate live fowls, with their legs tied together. They sit there quietly enough until she lowers the basket and lifts them out, a pair at a time for me to feel the weight.

It is very disagreeable to have to buy poultry alive, but the climate renders this absolutely necessary, as they can only be kept a very short time when killed.

'Well, how much for this pair?'

'Three and ninepence, missis, but I'll take three and six.'

The good creature knows my ways now and does the bating herself.

Annie Manville Fenn, Housekeeping in Jamaica, 16 March 1893

Not so many years ago, the usual way of buying fowls was from the market on Saturdays or, as described above, from the 'higgler' or itinerant vendor. Because of the lack of cooling facilities and refrigerators at the time, poultry was bought live and either kept in the yard to be fattened or, more usually, killed on Sunday morning for dinner.

A ritual surrounded the purchasing of poultry. The bird was held in one hand and 'weighed'; the craw was felt to make sure that it was not stuffed with corn, thus adding extra weight; the feet were also observed for signs of disease; and if the bird was a rooster, the comb was carefully checked for health – if it was red then it was healthy. These, then, were all country fowls. Their flavour was far superior to the battery-reared chicken we get today.

I remember two unusual birds from my childhood: first the sensey or sensa, a fowl with ruffled feathers whose name, according to Anderson and Cundall, comes from the Ashanti 'asense', and secondly the 'peel neck' fowl, whose neck was devoid of feathers. This was also known as Jack Panya or Panna (Spanish), which suggests its origin.

Still to be found, but not in great quantities, are ducks, turkeys, geese, guinea hens and peacocks. With the exception of duck, most of these birds are now rarely used in our cooking. The peacock may have been more popular in the past; Lady Nugent, in her journal of 25 November 1801, describes a dish served at a dinner given in honour of herself and her husband as 'One dish I shall never forget; it was a roasted peacock, placed before me, with all the feathers of the tail stuck in, and spread so naturally, that I expected every minute to see him strut out of the dish.'

There are many kinds of game bird – wild duck, teal, plover, ringtail pigeons, bald pates, ground and turtle doves – but the game bird population has declined drastically in recent years, and an attempt has been made to increase their numbers by allowing bird shooting for only a few months in the year. These birds are delicious stewed, fricasséed, made into pies, or grilled if they are tender.

### ✳PROVERB✳

Jack panna (peel neck) fowl cry fe life,
him no cry fe feddef (feather).
(Life is more important than the keeping up of appearances:
for if life be granted, appearances may be regained.)

## FRICASSÉED CHICKEN

1 chicken, 4 lb (2 kg)
juice of 1 lime
salt
black pepper, freshly ground if possible
1 clove garlic, crushed
1 sprig fresh thyme
2 onions, sliced
2 tomatoes, chopped

3–4 slices hot pepper, Scotch bonnet if possible, seeds removed
1 whole green hot pepper, Scotch bonnet if possible
¼ cup (2 fl oz, 50 ml) oil
2–3 cups (¾–1¼ pints, 500–750 ml) water

Wash and dry the chicken, removing any feathers still remaining on it. Rub it all over with the lime juice. Cut into joints and place them in a bowl. Season with salt and plenty of black pepper, and add the garlic, thyme, onions, tomatoes, slices of hot pepper and whole hot pepper. Mix well, ensuring that each piece of chicken is well coated. Leave the chicken to marinate for 15 minutes.

Remove the chicken pieces from the bowl, and fry in the oil (or a half-and-half mixture of oil and butter) over a moderate heat until very brown. Fry as many pieces as the pan will hold without overlapping, and when they are all browned, remove them from the pan. Take the pan off the heat for a minute or so for it to cool a little, then lower the heat, put the pan back, and scrape in the seasonings in which the chicken was marinated. Stir for a minute or so, then pour in the water, bring to the boil, and add the chicken pieces. Cover the pan and simmer for 1 hour or until the chicken is tender but not falling apart. Be careful not to break the whole hot pepper.

Taste the juices for salt and, if the gravy is too liquid, reduce it by increasing the heat, leaving the cover off, until the excess liquid evaporates. The juices from the chicken together with the seasonings will produce a thick delicious gravy; no thickening is ever needed, and if you do add any then this dish will lose much of its character. Remove the whole pepper carefully before serving.

I have eaten chicken prepared in many ways, but to my mind this is one of the most delicious ways of cooking it. It goes very well with rice and peas, fried plantains, avocado slices and a fresh salad. Enough for 4–5.

## CURRIED CHICKEN

| | |
|---|---|
| 1 chicken, 4 lb (2 kg) | 2 tomatoes, chopped |
| juice of 1 lime | 4 slices hot pepper, seeds removed |
| ¼ cup (2 fl oz, 50 ml) oil | 1 whole hot pepper (optional) |
| 2 onions, chopped | black pepper |
| 1 clove garlic, chopped | salt |
| 4 tablespoons curry powder (see p. 28) | 2–3 cups (¾–1¼ pints, 450–750 ml) water |

Wash and dry the chicken, rub it with the lime juice and cut it into small pieces. Lightly brown them, a few at a time, in oil or a mixture of oil and butter (the oil will prevent the butter from burning). Set the browned chicken aside in a bowl.

In the oil in which the chicken was browned, sauté the onions and garlic for a minute or so, then add the curry powder and stir. Throw in the tomatoes, hot pepper slices, whole pepper, black pepper and a little salt. Pour in the water, stir, and add the chicken pieces. Bring to the boil, then lower the heat, cover the pan, and simmer until the chicken is tender. Taste for salt just before the liquid is reduced to a gravy (approximately 1 hour). Serve it with the usual accompaniments to a curried dish. Serves 4–5.

## BAKED PIGEONS OR BALD PATES

pigeons *or* bald pates          black pepper
lime juice                       1 slice bacon for each bird
salt                             butter

If your pigeons or bald pates are not plucked and drawn, then prepare them by pouring some boiling water over them. In a few minutes, the hot water will allow the feathers to be removed easily. Pluck them, cut off the heads, then make an incision in the lower abdomen and remove and discard the entrails.

Wash the birds thoroughly, dry them, and rub them with lime juice. Sprinkle salt and pepper over them and wrap each in a slice of bacon. Place the birds, side by side, in a baking pan and place them in a moderate oven – 350°F, 180°C, gas 4. They will take about 1 hour to cook, during which time they should be basted every so often with the juices from the pan, to which a little butter has been added. When they are brown on one side turn them over. As soon as they are done, remove them to a serving dish and keep warm.

Add some water to the juices in the pan, scraping and amalgamating any drippings that have stuck to the pan. Let the gravy reduce, and serve it separately from the birds. Serve the birds arranged on a large platter decorated with some parsley or watercress, accompanied by a purée of sweet potatoes, baked plantains, rice, avocado slices, and a salad.

# FRICASSÉE OF GAME BIRDS

Game birds brought back from a shoot provide a welcome change from the usual fare, but these little birds can at times be extremely tough. I find that cooking them very slowly in a 'dutch pot' or heavy braising pan ensures that they become tender.

| | |
|---|---|
| game birds | onions, chopped |
| salt | garlic, chopped |
| black pepper | tomatoes, chopped |
| oil | hot pepper |
| butter | thyme sprigs |

Pluck and prepare the birds as described in the previous recipe, but in addition be sure to remove the pellets that have burrowed into the flesh. Season the birds with salt and black pepper. Brown them in some oil and butter, then remove from the pan and set aside while you make the sauce.

Fry some chopped onions and garlic in the oil and butter in which the birds were fried, then add chopped tomatoes, hot pepper, thyme, salt and pepper to taste. Pour in just enough water to cover the birds, stir, bring to the boil, then lower the heat and arrange the birds in the pan. Cover and simmer until the birds are tender (about 1–2 hours depending on how tough they are) and the juices reduced to a nice gravy.

If there is still too much liquid when the birds are done, remove them from the pan, keep them warm, and reduce the gravy by rapid boiling. Pour the gravy over the birds and serve immediately.

# ROAST DUCK

A nicely roasted duck is not often encountered. This method ensures that the bird comes out tender and juicy.

| | |
|---|---|
| 1 duck, 4–5 lb (2–2.5 kg), with giblets | pepper |
| 4 cups (1½ pints, 1 litre) water | 1 bouquet of herbs – thyme, celery, parsley, tied together |
| 1 carrot, sliced | small piece tangerine or Seville orange peel, chopped |
| 1 whole onion | |
| 1 tomato, chopped | 1 onion, chopped |
| salt | 2–3 slices hot pepper, chopped |

Duck produces a large amount of fat, which must be got rid of. The duck is then basted with a stock made from the giblets.

Put the giblets in a small pan and add the water, carrot, whole onion, tomato, salt and pepper and the bouquet of herbs. Bring to the boil, then simmer for 1 hour. Prepare this stock before roasting the duck.

When the stock is ready, place the duck on its side in a roasting pan. Season it with salt and pepper and cook it for 30 minutes in a preheated oven at 325°F, 160°C, gas 3. By this time a lot of fat will have accumulated in the pan; skim this off and pour in the stock. Turn the bird on to its other side and leave it in the oven for a further 30 minutes, basting it from time to time with the stock. When both sides are done, turn the duck on its back, with the breast upwards, until it is brown. The bird should take about 1¼–1½ hours to cook in all.

Pour the sauce from the roasting pan into a small pan, skimming off any excess fat, and heat it quickly, adding the peel, chopped onion, hot pepper and salt if necessary.

Transfer the duck to a serving platter with some sprigs of parsley, and serve the sauce separately in a bowl. Baked or puréed sweet potatoes, fried plantains and avocado slices are good accompaniments for this rich-flavoured fowl.

# ROAST GUINEA FOWL

| | |
|---|---|
| 1 guinea fowl | black pepper |
| salt | butter |

The guinea fowl was brought to the West Indies from Africa. It is not a very common bird now, although one occasionally sees a few roaming about in yards both in Kingston and in the country areas. I have never seen any for sale, so presumably the owners keep them for their own use. The flavour of the meat lies between the gamey flavour of a pheasant and chicken. It tends to be a rather dry meat, so care is needed in its preparation.

Season the bird inside and out with salt and black pepper. Rub it liberally with butter and place it on its side on a piece of foil large enough to enclose it. Fold over the edges in order to seal in the juices. Bake in a hot oven, 400°F, 200°C, gas 6, for 30 minutes, then remove the foil, leaving the bird on its side in the roasting pan with any juice that has accumulated in the foil. Let it brown on one side then the other, basting it with its own juice, to which you might have to add a little water from time to time. It should take about 1¼ hours to cook in all.

Serve the bird on a large platter, accompanied by its own sauce in a separate bowl. A purée of sweet potatoes goes well with it.

# BREAD AND BUNS

# *BREAD

We have a long history of bread-making, dating back to the time of the Arawak Indians. The zabi or bammy, their most cherished food, has survived the centuries and is today made in almost exactly the same way as that described by Oviedo in his *Natural History of the West Indies*, written in the early sixteenth century:

There is another kind of bread that is called *cazabi* which is made from the root of a plant the Indians call yuca . . . In order to make bread of it which is called cassava, the Indians grate it and then press it in a strainer, which is a sort of sack about ten palms or more in length and as big as a man's leg. The Indians make this bag from palms which are woven together as if they were rushes. By twisting the strainer as one does to remove the milk from crushed almonds, the juice is extracted from the yuca. This juice is a powerful and deadly poison, and one swallow of it will produce sudden death.

The residue after the liquid is removed, which is something like moist bran, is cooked in the fire in a very hot, flat clay vessel of the size they want the loaf to be. The mash is spread out, taking care that none of the liquid remains in it, then a loaf of the desired size is formed, which is necessarily the same size as the vessel in which it is baked. When the loaf has become firm it is removed from the fire and cured. Often it is placed in the sun. The Indians then eat it for it is very good bread. The liquid which is extracted from the yuca is boiled several times and left in the open for several days. Then it becomes sweet and used as honey or other syrup to mix with other foods. Later this liquid is boiled and placed outdoors. It then turns sour and is used for vinegar without danger whatsoever to the user.

This cassava bread can be kept for a year or more and can be carried from one place to another, even great distances without spoiling or becoming stale. It is good food for sea voyages and it is carried by the Indians on all their trips, to the islands and to Terra Firme, without becoming bad or soggy.

The species of poisonous yuca grows in great abundance on the islands of San Juan, Cuba, Jamaica and Hispaniola. There is another species called boniata,* the juice of which is not poisonous. This species is eaten after it has been cooked like carrots with or without wine, and is very good bread.

* The sweet cassava.

The cassava plant, a native of the New World tropics, was introduced into Asia and Africa by the colonizing powers as early as the seventeenth century and has become an important staple in the diet of many tropical countries.

Yeast-leavened bread was a late introduction to Jamaica, and until the middle of the nineteenth century bicarbonate of soda was used as the leavening agent. Fresh yeast had a short life span in the days before refrigeration, and it was probably only after compressed yeast was developed that yeast-leavened breads made their appearance in Jamaica.

The most popular all-purpose bread in Jamaica is commercially produced 'hard-dough' – a dense, solid bread, as the name suggests. It makes excellent toast, but it is usually eaten simply spread with butter or margarine. It is not a bread that can easily be made in the home.

Here are a few of the soda-leavened bread recipes which are still popular, and a bammy recipe.

### ✳PROVERB✳

If you want half a bread beg s'mody buy it,
but if you want hole a wan, buy it yourself.
(If you want a thing well done, do it yourself.)

## BAMMY

Fried fish and bammies are the specialities of the fishing town Old Harbour, on the south coast. Near the market and the clock tower, ladies are strategically positioned on the piazzas with their 'show cases'. From here they shout 'Fry fish and bammy' at passing cars. The delicacies are neatly arranged in the show case and prospective customers can choose what they like. Nearby, other vendors are busy disposing of the day's catch of fish to eager buyers who have come from as far away as Kingston.

Travelling west on the south coast one comes to a point near the town of Black River where the call to the passing cars is 'Pepper shrimps'. These are the river crayfish which have been cooked and heavily salted – they are also very 'peppery' hot. Some of these ladies also sell the famous St Elizabeth bammies, which are much larger than the normal ones.

| | |
|---|---|
| 2 lb (1 kg) sweet cassava *or* 4 cups | 1 teaspoon salt |
| (1½ lb, 750 g) grated cassava | |

Peel and grate the cassava. Place it in a muslin cloth and wring out and discard as much of the juice as possible. Add the salt to the cassava 'bran'. Place about a cup of the mixture in a greased shallow baking pan or frying pan, or, if you can get hold of some of the tin rings used for making bammies, fill these with the same amount. Press down with the bottom of a bottle or a similar implement. The bammies should be about 6 inches (15 cm) in diameter.

Place the pan over a moderate heat. In a few minutes, as the pan heats up, some steam will rise. When the edges shrink slightly from the sides of the pan, flatten the mixture and turn it over to cook the other side. Each bammy should take about 10 minutes in all. Repeat the process until all the cassava is used up. At this stage the bammies can be kept in the fridge for up to 4 days, or frozen until needed.

When you are ready to use the bammies, soak them in some milk for about 10 minutes and either fry them in oil or grill them until they are golden brown. Butter them, and serve hot with any dish.

RIDDLE:  'Mi fader hab a whole patch of cassava; one white belly rat eat it off.'
ANSWER:  A cassava grater.

## JOHNNY CAKES

| | |
|---|---|
| 3 cups (1 lb, 500 g) flour | 2 tablespoons (1 oz, 30 g) butter |
| 2 teaspoons baking powder | oil |
| 1 teaspoon salt | |

Sift together the flour, baking powder and salt. Mix in the butter and add enough water to make a stiff dough. Shape into 2-inch

(5-cm) balls and deep fry them in moderately hot oil until they are brown. They are delicious with butter and are usually served at breakfast with, for example, escoveitch fish, or as a light meal with meat. They are also known as journey cakes, as they are ideal travellers' snacks. Caroline Sullivan (*Jamaica Cookery Book*, 1893) knew them in a flattened, round form, about ½ inch (1 cm) thick, baked on a grid.

## CORN BREAD

| | |
|---|---|
| 1 cup (6 oz, 175 g) flour | 4 tablespoons sugar |
| 2 teaspoons baking powder | 2 eggs, beaten |
| 1 teaspoon salt | 1 cup (8 fl oz, 250 ml) milk |
| 1 cup (6 oz, 175 g) cornmeal | ¼ cup (2 oz, 50 g) softened butter |

Sift together the flour, baking powder and salt, then add the cornmeal and sugar. Stir in the beaten eggs, milk and butter, mixing well until the batter is smooth. Pour it into a greased loaf tin and bake in a moderately hot oven, 350°F, 180°C, gas 4, for 25–30 minutes or until golden brown.

## ❋SWEET BREADS AND BUNS

Included in this section are many of the old favourite sweet breads and buns, evoking happy memories of events now long past and still a daily source of pleasure and satisfaction. They are easy to make, and the majority need only baking powder as a raising agent. Sweet breads are eaten as snacks, at teatime or for dessert, and sometimes at breakfast. Try them with avocado – the combination is delicious.

## COCONUT BREAD

4 cups (1½ lb, 600 g) flour
2 teaspoons baking powder
½ teaspoon salt
2 cups (8 oz, 250 g) grated coconut (use desiccated if fresh not available)

¾ cup (6 oz, 175 g) sugar
1 teaspoon vanilla
1 egg, beaten
1 cup (8 fl oz, 250 ml) milk
sugar for dusting

Sift together the flour, baking powder and salt. Add the coconut, sugar, vanilla and beaten egg, beating the mixture well after each addition.

Pour in the milk a little at a time, until the dough is firm but not sticky. (Add a little more flour should it become so.) Knead the dough for a few minutes, then shape it into loaves to fit your greased loaf tins to about three-quarters of their height.

Dust the top with fine sugar and bake in a moderately hot oven, 350°F, 180°C, gas 4, for 1 hour or until golden brown.

## BANANA BREAD

2 cups (10 oz, 300 g) flour
3 teaspoons baking powder
½ teaspoon salt
½ teaspoon nutmeg
½ cup (4 oz, 125 g) butter

1 cup (8 oz, 250 g) sugar
1 egg, beaten
3 very ripe bananas
½ cup (4 fl oz, 125 ml) milk
1 teaspoon vanilla

Sift together the flour, baking powder, salt and nutmeg, and set aside.

Cream the butter and sugar. When the mixture takes on a very pale, satiny sheen, add the beaten egg and the bananas, mashed to a smooth paste. Mix well after each addition. Add the flour gradually with the milk, and lastly add the vanilla. The mixture should be thick but not too stiff. Pour it into a greased loaf or bread tin and bake it in a moderately hot oven, 350°F, 180°C, gas 4, for 1 hour or until brown. Test by inserting a long skewer or knife in the centre – if it is ready the knife or skewer will come out clean. If not, bake it for a little while longer.

# COCONUT BUNS

| | |
|---|---|
| 1 teaspoon baking powder | 1 egg, beaten |
| 1½ cups (7 oz, 225 g) flour | 1 cup (4 oz, 125 g) grated coconut |
| ½ cup (4 oz, 125 g) butter | milk |
| ¾ cup (6 oz, 175 g) sugar | |

Sift together the baking powder and flour. Cream the butter and sugar until the mixture is light and fluffy; add the beaten egg, then mix in the flour and coconut alternately with enough milk to produce a thick mixture. Drop spoonfuls on to a greased baking sheet, and bake in a moderately hot oven, 350°F, 180°C, gas 4, for 30 minutes or until they are brown.

# THE EASTER BUN

Spiced fruit buns were the original Good Friday hot cross buns which became very popular during Tudor days in England.

They are still eaten at Easter time in England, and some of the Yorkshire buns are identical to our Easter buns. In Jamaica, Easter bun is eaten with cheese.

| | |
|---|---|
| ¾ oz (20 g) dry yeast or 1½ oz (40 g) fresh yeast | 4 oz (125 g) cherries |
| | 1 cup (6 oz, 175 g) brown sugar |
| 1 cup (8 fl oz, 250 ml) hot milk | 1 nutmeg, freshly grated or 1 |
| 1 cup (8 oz, 250 g) butter | tablespoon powdered nutmeg |
| 6 cups (2 lb, 900 g) flour | 1 teaspoon ground cinnamon |
| 4 oz (125 g) raisins | 1 teaspoon salt |
| 4 oz (125 g) currants | 1 egg, beaten |
| 4 oz (125 g) chopped citron | 4 tablespoons molasses |

Dissolve the yeast in a small amount of water, just warm enough to sting slightly when tested on the inside of the wrist. Leave for 10 minutes until it becomes frothy. In the meantime heat the milk and add the butter. Remove the pan from the heat as soon as the butter melts, stir, and set aside.

Sieve the flour into a large mixing bowl. Add the yeast liquid and the fruit, mixing well after each addition. To the milk and butter mixture, add the sugar, nutmeg, cinnamon, salt, beaten egg and molasses. Combine this gradually with the flour mixture, adding just enough to make a dough that is not sticky.

Knead well and leave to rise for 2 hours, then knead once again. Shape into loaves of whatever size you wish. Place small loaves on greased baking sheets, larger ones in bread tins, and leave them to rise again for approximately 1 hour. Bake the loaves in a pre-heated slow oven at 300–325°F, 150–180°C, gas 2–4. As soon as they begin to turn brown, paint them with a glaze made from a mixture of molasses or sugar and water and bake for a further 15 minutes or so.

The buns are cooked when a skewer inserted into the middle comes out clean. (Large ones should take 45–60 minutes, small ones about 30 minutes, in all.) Cool the buns before taking them out of their tins.


## BULLAS

These round flat cakes were very popular at one time. They used to be made by the small bakers in the towns, from whose shops would float the smell of fresh bread and the sweet spicy odours of these cakes. Crispy outside, soft inside, they were eaten hot with avocado pear and freshly made lemonade.

Unfortunately these cakes almost disappeared for many years, no doubt owing to the monopoly of the large modern bakeries and the extinction of many small ones. They are beginning to reappear in the shops, but the commercially produced ones are not a patch on those freshly baked.

3 cups (1 lb, 450 g) flour
2 teaspoons baking powder
½ teaspoon salt
1 teaspoon nutmeg
½ teaspoon ground pimento
   (allspice)

1 teaspoon grated fresh ginger
3 tablespoons melted butter
1 cup (8 oz, 250 g) sugar,
   dissolved in 1 cup (8 fl oz,
   250 ml) water

Sift together the flour, baking powder, salt, nutmeg and pimento. Mix in the grated ginger, melted butter, and enough of the sugar and water solution to make a firm dough.

Knead the dough vigorously for 5 minutes, then roll it out on a floured board to about ½ inch (1 cm) in thickness. Using a small saucer, cut out circles in the dough. Lift each circle off the board with a spatula, and dust on both sides with some flour. Bake them on a greased baking sheet, in a preheated oven at 375°F, 190°C, gas 5, for about 30 minutes. They are best eaten hot, but they should keep for up to a week.

## TOTOES

These are analogous to the Eastern Caribbean 'bake', though somewhat sweeter. They are eaten in the same way as bullas.

| | |
|---|---|
| ½ cup (4 oz, 125 g) butter | ½ teaspoon nutmeg |
| 1 cup (8 oz, 250 g) sugar | 1 egg, beaten |
| 2 cups (10 oz, 300 g) flour | 1 teaspoon vanilla |
| 2 teaspoons baking powder | milk |
| 1 teaspoon powdered cinnamon | |

Cream the butter with the sugar until the mixture is light and fluffy. Sift together the flour, baking powder, cinnamon and nutmeg, and gradually add to the butter and sugar. Lastly add the beaten egg, the vanilla and just sufficient milk to make the mixture into a stiff paste.

Transfer the mixture to a greased, shallow baking tin, making sure that it is evenly spread. Bake in a preheated oven at 400°F, 200°C, gas 6, for 1 hour or until brown. Cut into pieces when cool.

## GINGERBREAD

Jamaica produces the finest ginger in the world. It has a subtle, mild flavour which is highly prized by connoisseurs world-wide.

This is a very old recipe for gingerbread.

| | |
|---|---|
| ½ cup (4 fl oz, 125 ml) molasses | 2 teaspoons baking powder |
| 1 cup (8 oz, 250 g) sugar | ½ teaspoon salt |
| ½ cup (4 oz, 125 g) butter | 1 teaspoon nutmeg |
| ½ cup (4 fl oz, 125 ml) hot water | 2 teaspoons grated fresh ginger |
| 2 cups (10 oz, 300 g) flour | 1 egg, beaten |

Heat the molasses, sugar and butter gently in a pan. Pour in the hot water, mix well, and set aside.

Sift together the flour, baking powder, salt and nutmeg, then add the grated ginger and the well beaten egg. Combine the molasses liquid with the flour mixture, and pour the resulting batter into a shallow tin lined with greased paper. Bake in a slow oven at 300–350°F, 150–160°C, gas 2–3, for 1 hour or until done.

# DESSERTS

Pineapple

Water coconut

Paw Paw

Star apple

Soursop

Mango

Grapefruit

Lime

Ugli

Lemon

Mandarine

Banana

Sea Grapes

Cashew nuts

Guava

I was at first surprised when I realized that 500 of the 900 recipes I had collected during my research fell into the category of sweets or desserts, yet when I thought about it this no longer seemed surprising. There is no doubt that we have the proverbial 'sweet tooth', and this is understandable since for a very long time sugar has been our *raison d'être*, a commodity that has affected us and our history deeply in many ways.

Almost all our puddings, cakes and tarts have their origin in English and European cooking, but one transplant that has remained with us from Africa is 'duckunoo', also known as 'blue drawers', a dough made from cornmeal, sugar and spices which is wrapped in banana leaves and boiled.

Not so many years ago it was a common sight to see, gracefully walking down the street, itinerant vendors with large glass containers precariously balanced on their heads. Peeping through the glass cases was an exciting assortment of iced pink and white cakes, gizadas, plantain tarts and various puddings. These vendors made their way from house to house, to those regular customers whom they had acquired over the years. Annie Manville Fenn, in *Housekeeping in Jamaica* (1893), describes such a visit:

The next arrival, with a kind of double tray, is the cake woman. The top tray contains Jamaica sweet-meats – peppermint sticks and other tooth-destroying delicacies. She removes this and underneath are various kinds of spongy cakes and small basins of preserved pine, mango, watermelon or other fruit. These confections are made, I am told, by Jewish ladies who employ the black women as sellers. I believe they do a thriving trade, especially with the hotels and lodging houses.

It is now the groceries, bakeries and supermarkets that sell buns, cakes, tarts and so on, but, as always, the best are baked at home.

From the large number of recipes collected for this section I have chosen a representative selection, giving preference to those which make the best use of local products and those whose ingredients are readily available.

# *FRUIT AND FRUIT DESSERTS

Jamaica is blessed with an abundance of the most delicious fruits. Throughout the year the markets provide a selection of the fruits in season, and roadside stalls offer the traveller an attractive display of citrus fruit tied to sticks, baskets piled high with mangoes, otaheite apples or naseberries, hands of ripe bananas, and long sticks of sugar cane which the vendor will cut into convenient lengths and peel for the buyer to chew. The sweet juice is sucked out of the stick and the trash thrown away.

Fruit is eaten at any time of the day and used rarely to be served at the end of a meal, dessert being a cooked or prepared dish. This has changed, and now many menus will include a selection of fresh fruit as a dessert.

Here is a list of our main fruits.

## BANANA
See p. 59.

## CASHEW

The cashew (*Anacardium occidentale*) is a native of the American tropics but is now grown throughout the tropical world. The fruit is pear-shaped and the seed or nut is attached to the bottom.

Though the fruit is tart and slightly astringent in taste, the juice makes a delicious cooling drink. Cashews are also made into a lovely highly perfumed preserve. In other countries a vinegar is made from the juice, and when fermented it produces a wine which is famous in Brazil.

The outer skin of the nut (really a hard shell) contains an oily fuel. When the nuts are thrown among live charcoals they blaze, and care has to be taken to stop them burning to cinders. Of course, the nuts are also commercially roasted.

## CITRUS

### GRAPEFRUIT
*C. paradisi*, of West Indian origin, possibly from Jamaica.

### LEMON
*C. limon*, native of S. E. Asia. The fruits are generally larger in Jamaica than those available in the U.K.

### LIME
*C. aurantifolia*. The fruits are light yellow when ripe, but are usually

picked green as they go bad quickly when very ripe. They are very sour, smaller than lemons and with a stronger, fresher flavour. If you can get them abroad, use them instead of lemons. They make excellent lemonade.

### MANDARINES, TANGERINES

*C. reticulata,* native of China. The fruits are easily peeled. They are eaten fresh, but also made into jellies and marmalades and used as flavouring for liqueurs.

### ORTANIQUE

This Jamaican invention is a cross between a tangerine and an orange. The fruit is the size of an orange and has the colour of the tangerine.

### SEVILLE OR SOUR ORANGE

*C. vulgaris,* a native of S. E. Asia, makes excellent marmalades and liqueurs, and is used to flavour sauces.

### SHADDOCK

*C. grandis,* native of S. E. Asia. The fruit is 4–12 inches (10–30 cm) long, weighing at times as much as 4 lb (2 kg). It is rough-skinned, green to yellow in colour, with pink flesh.

### SWEET ORANGE

*C. sinensis,* native of China. Many varieties are grown.

### UGLI

This is a cross between a grapefruit and a tangerine. It is rough-skinned, pink-fleshed, and about the size of a grapefruit.

## COCONUT

The coconut (*Cocos mucifera*) is a member of the palm family of plants. It is a native of the Old World tropics and was introduced here during the Spanish period. The water inside the immature nut is a favourite cooling drink, and doctors often advise patients with gallstone and kidney problems to drink it. It is often confused with coconut milk, which is made by adding water to grated coconut and pressing through a sieve. Coconut milk is an important flavouring in dishes such as rice and peas, and also makes a good ice cream. The coconut flesh is made into chips and candies. Use a heavy implement such as a hammer to break the hard shell of the coconut.

## COOLIE PLUM (JUJUBE, CRAB APPLE)

The coolie plum (*Ziziphus mauritiana*) is a native of the tropical Old World, but is now found throughout the West Indies and elsewhere in the tropics. The fruit is small, brownish-orange in colour and tart – it is a favourite with children.

## CUSTARD APPLE (BULLOCK'S HEART)

The custard apple (*A. rectulata*) is a member of the Annoan family. It is a native of the New World tropics and has been introduced into the Old World tropics. It is often made into a delicious drink or dessert or into ice cream.

## GARDEN CHERRY (ACEROLA, BARBADOS CHERRY, WEST INDIAN CHERRY)

The garden cherry (*Malpighia punicifolia*) is a small, red, tart berry which is very rich in Vitamin C, and appears to be of West Indian origin. The fruit has a lot of pith inside; when crushed it makes a wonderful drink, sorbet or jelly.

## GUAVA

The guava (*Psidium guajava*) is a round thin-skinned fruit, a few inches long, with many seeds. The flesh is usually yellow to bright pink in colour and highly perfumed. It is delicious stewed, and is also made into drinks, jellies, jams and sweets. It is available tinned in the U.K.

## GUINEP

The fruits of the guinep (*Allophylus paniculata*) appear in grape-like bunches on the tree. They are round, green and rough-skinned on the outside with a pink pulp on a large seed. The flavour is not unlike that of lychees. It is a native of Brazil and is known in Barbados as ackee. A favourite fruit with children.

## HOG PLUM

This tree (*Spondias mombin*) is a native of the New World tropics. It is not cultivated, but found along roadsides. The fruit is oval, yellow and a couple of inches long, with not much pulp on the large seed. It is usually made into jellies.

## JEW PLUM (JUNE PLUM)

This plant (*Spondias dulcis*) is a native of the South Pacific. The fruit is yellow when ripe, about 3 inches (7.5 cm) long, with a sweet, pungent flavour. The flesh is arranged around a shiny fibrous seed. It is made into jams and pickles.

## MAMMEY (MAMMEE) APPLE

This tree (*Mammea americana*) is a native of the New World tropics. The fruit is sometimes as large as a grapefruit. The outer skin is brown and rough, and the edible pulp is yellow/tangerine in colour and recalls the flavour of peaches. It is usually made into jam.

## MANGO

Jamaicans have a passion for mangoes and eat them in abundance during the summer months when they are in season. Sometimes mangoes will replace a whole meal.

The mango (*Manfifera indica*) is a native of India. In June 1782 several varieties of mango were found on board a French ship bound for Hispaniola. The ship was intercepted by H.M.S. *Flora*, one of Lord Rodney's squadrons, and the mangoes were sent as a prize to Jamaica. They were planted in the botanical gardens of a Mr East at Liguanea.

There are many varieties in the island, differing in shape, colour, texture, size and taste. The most esteemed are the hybrids, the Bombay, the St Julian and the East Indian.

Mangoes are best eaten fresh but can also be juiced, made into ice cream, tarts and other desserts.

## NASEBERRY (SAPODILLA)

The naseberry (*Manilkara zapota*) is a native of the tropical Americas. The fruit is small, round or oval shaped, brown-skinned and 2 inches (5 cm) or so long. The flesh is also brown, very sweet, and tastes somewhat like dates. Naseberries are usually to be found for sale along the St Thomas road going east towards Portland. They are best eaten fresh, and are often added to fruit salad.

## OTAHEITE APPLE

This tree (*Syzygium malaccense*) is native to Malaya and was introduced from the Pacific by Captain Bligh in the eighteenth century. The fruit is pear-shaped, 2–4 inches (5–10 cm) long, and pink to ruby red in colour. The flesh is white, crisp and delicately perfumed. It is usually eaten fresh.

## PASSION FRUIT (SWEET CUP)

The passion fruit vine (*Passifloracea edulis*) bears fruit 2–3 inches (5–8 cm) long, most often green/yellow in colour and hard-shelled. When opened the fruit shows a mass of seeds surrounded by a fleshy pulp. It makes an excellent drink, and the juice is sought after for the making of ice creams, mousses and sorbets.

## PAWPAW (PAPAYA)

There are two varieties of pawpaw. The first, *Carica jamaicensis*, is endemic and bears clusters of 1–6 small yellow fruit. The second, *C. papaya*, produces the large fruit; this is also a native of the American tropics, and was introduced into Africa and many other tropical countries. It is best eaten fresh with a squeeze of lime juice. It also makes a delicious drink or nectar. It is available abroad tinned.

## PINEAPPLE

The pineapple (*Ananas comosus*) is native to the Guyanas and Brazil.

It has been grown in Jamaica for a very long time and is called 'pine' here. The best eating variety is called the sugar loaf. It is best eaten fresh.

## ROSE APPLE

The rose apple tree (*Syzygium jambos*) grows wild along streams, especially in the hills around Kingston, but is, however, a native of the Indo-Malaysian region. The fruit is small, round, yellow in colour when ripe, with a large seed inside. The flesh has a distinctive taste of roses. It makes a lovely preserve, although it is usually eaten fresh.

## SEA GRAPE

The sea grape (*Coccoloba uvifera*) is found as a shrub or tree growing near the sea. The fruit appears in grape-like bunches, and each is about 1 inch (2 cm) long, round and purple in colour, with a slightly salty yet sweet taste. It makes a lovely jelly, but is more often eaten fresh.

## SOURSOP

The soursop fruit (*Annonaceae muricata*) is native to the American tropics. It is heart-shaped, some 6–8 inches (15–20 cm) long, with soft spiky projections all over the green skin. The flesh is white and highly perfumed, and makes a delicious drink and ice cream. It is said to be eaten for its tranquillizing effect.

## STAR APPLE (CARAMBOLA, KAIMET)

The star apple (*Chrysophyllum cainito*) is native to the islands of the Greater Antilles, although it is now found in other tropical countries. The leaves of this beautiful tall tree are green above and bronze underneath. The fruit is green or purple, the size of an apple or orange. When cut across, the fruit has a star-shaped arrangement of pulp and seeds, hence the name.

The fruit must be soft when squeezed, otherwise it will be dry inside. It is eaten on its own, raw, and mixed with oranges in a beautiful dessert called matrimony.

## SWEETSOP

The fruit of the sweetsop (*Annonaceae squamosa*) is 2–3 inches (5–8 cm) wide and green when ripe, with rough indented skin. The fruit is made up of many black seeds, each surrounded by a white pulp which is very sweet. The shrub is native to the tropical Americas but is now found in many other countries.

## TAMARIND

The tamarind (*Tamarindus indica*) is a native of East Africa or S. Asia and it grows wild in India. The fruit or pod is stripped of its hard outer shell, and is usually preserved or made into a cooling drink or a sweet called tamarind balls.

## FRUIT SALAD

bananas, oranges and other fruits     sugar (optional)
  in season

Whatever other fruits one uses, I think a salad should include bananas and oranges or grapefruit.

Peel and slice the bananas and place them in a bowl. Peel the oranges and/or grapefruit, cut into segments, remove the pith and inner skins, and place the flesh on top of the bananas. If the citrus fruits are not juicy then squeeze one orange and a lime over the bananas to prevent them turning black. Add any other fruit, peeled and cut into small pieces. Add sugar if desired, and keep refrigerated until required.

Alternatively, a light syrup can be poured over the fruit salad instead of sugar. Make the syrup from 1 cup of water, 1 cup of sugar and the juice of one lime; bring to the boil, reduce the heat and simmer until it lightly coats a spoon. Cool before using.

## MATRIMONY

I find it difficult to describe the texture and taste of this dessert. Suffice it to say that it is a most sensuously smooth dessert, purple and white or milky white, depending on whether one uses the green-skinned or the purple star apple.

The star apple season is relatively short, from February to April, and one looks forward to it if one is passionately addicted to these fruit. This is the time of the year when there is also an abundance of citrus.

4 large star apples         nutmeg
3 oranges                sugar
2 cups (¾ pint, 500 ml) milk

If you cut the bottoms off the star apples, less than half-way down, you will see the perfect star shape in the fruit. Scoop out the soft pulp, leaving behind the harder part near the skin. Pick out the seeds and discard them if you wish, although I find that they are very beautiful to look at, and usually leave them in.

Peel the oranges, cut them into segments, remove the pith and inner skins and add the flesh to the star apples. Refrigerate until the dish is to be served, then add the milk, grate some nutmeg over the top and add enough sugar to sweeten. The milk is added at the last moment to prevent curdling. Enough for 4.


## ANGEL'S FOOD

This is a very appropriate name for the unusual combination of oranges and grated coconut.

6 oranges                                       1 dry (mature) coconut

Peel the oranges, cut into segments and remove the white pith and inner skins. Grate the coconut after removing the dark outer skin. Arrange the orange segments in a glass bowl and sprinkle the grated coconut on top. Enough for 4.


## BANANAS AND CREAM

Bananas seem to have an unusual affinity with cream.

bananas                                         sugar
cream

Slice as many bananas as you wish, pour some cream over them, and over the cream sprinkle some sugar. Serve immediately.

## BAKED BANANAS

12 bananas
¼ cup (2 oz, 50 g) butter
½ teaspoon grated nutmeg

1 cup (6 oz, 175 g) brown sugar
1 cup (8 fl oz, 250 ml) water

Peel the bananas and place them in a long ovenproof dish. Dot them with the butter, grate the nutmeg over them, sprinkle with the sugar and add the water. Either bake them in a moderately hot oven until they are brown, or grill them, turning them over once.

Serve them with coconut cream (see p. 142). Enough for 6.

## STEWED CASHEWS

cashews
salt

sugar
nutmeg

Remove the nut from the fruit. Prick the fruit all over with a skewer and squeeze out the juice. (Use the juice for cashew wine, p. 172.) Care must be taken as the juice stains. Put the cashew fruit in a large bowl, add a little salt to get rid of the astringent taste, and leave them to drain for about 1 hour. Squeeze, wash and weigh them, and put them in a large pan with an equal quantity of sugar. Add ½ teaspoon of grated nutmeg and enough water to cover the cashews. Boil them until they are tender and the syrup thickens. Serve them at room temperature with coconut cream (see p. 142).

## STEWED GUAVAS

2 dozen guavas
2 cups (1 lb, 500 g) sugar

½ teaspoon nutmeg (optional)

Peel the guavas, cut them in half, and carefully scoop out the pulp and seeds. Place the guava shells in a pan with enough water just to cover them. Add the sugar, and the nutmeg if desired. Tie the seeds and pulp in a piece of muslin and drop this into the pan. Cook the guavas until they are tender and the syrup thickens.

Remove the pan from the heat, lift out the muslin bag, and discard.

Serve these delicious stewed guavas with coconut cream (see below). Enough for 4–5.

## STEWED OTAHEITE APPLE

otaheite apples                     lime juice
sugar

These red pear-shaped fruit are really best eaten fresh, but they can be preserved when there is an abundance.

Cut the fruit in half and remove the seed. Place the fruit in a pan with half their weight in sugar. For each 1 lb (500 g) of fruit add the juice of half a lime. Cover the fruit with water and cook until they are tender and the syrup thickens.

Serve with coconut cream (see next recipe).

## COCONUT CREAM

3 mature coconuts                     6 cups (2½ pints, 1.5 litres) water

Grate the coconuts, add the water, and mix thoroughly. Strain the liquid through muslin (or a sieve). Place the strained liquid in the refrigerator for 30 minutes. The cream will float to the top – skim this off into a bowl and serve immediately with your dessert

## BANANA FRITTERS

A good way of using up very ripe bananas.

6 very ripe bananas                     flour
2 eggs, beaten                              oil
½ teaspoon grated nutmeg           sugar

Peel the bananas and mash to a smooth paste. Add the beaten eggs, nutmeg and just enough flour to make a thick mixture. Fry the mixture in moderately hot oil, dropping it in by the spoonful. When the fritters are brown on one side, turn them over. Drain them on absorbent paper, arrange them on a large platter, and sprinkle them with some sugar.

## JELLY

The most delicious jellies can be made from unflavoured gelatine and the juice of almost any fruit. These jellies will be a far cry from the commercially packaged and artificially flavoured ones. Try making some with a combination of juices or with fresh fruit set in the jelly.

Use juices such as tangerine, soursop, tamarind, guava, garden cherry and pineapple (the latter, if fresh, must be heated, as there is a chemical in it which will not allow the jelly to set).

½ cup (4 fl oz, 125 ml) water
3 tablespoons gelatine
5 cups (2 pints, 1.25 litres) any
    fruit juice

½–1 cup (4–8 oz, 125–250 g)
    sugar (depending on the
    sweetness of the juice)
fruit (optional)

Heat the water, sprinkle in the gelatine, and stir until it has completely dissolved. Remove from the heat and add the juice, stirring well again. Taste, then add sugar if necessary and stir again until this has dissolved. If you are going to add fruit to the jelly, refrigerate three-quarters of the mixture in a jelly mould until it has set. Arrange whatever fruit you are using on top of the set jelly, pour the remaining juice over it, and return it to the refrigerator to set. Otherwise, place the whole mixture to set in the refrigerator.

Gelatines are made from either animal or vegetable sources. All the commercially packaged ones are animal-based, and 100 per cent protein. You can also prepare your own gelatine as shown in the following two recipes.

## COWFOOT JELLY

Cowfoot jelly is made from the gelatinous stock produced from the boiling of the cow's foot in the preparation of cowfoot and beans (see p. 98).

Having poured off the excess liquid from the cooked cow's foot, strain it through a piece of muslin. Add to it sugar, nutmeg, rum, some milk, and some strawberry syrup to colour it pink. Refrigerate until it has set. This makes a light, delicate jelly.

## IRISH MOSS

This jelly is of vegetable substances, made from a seaweed, *Graciliaria vellucosa*, which is popularly known as Irish moss. It is reputed to have aphrodisiac properties, but this is possibly in the mind rather than in the content.

| | |
|---|---|
| ½ lb (250 g) fresh *or* 2 oz (50 g) dried Irish moss | 1 tablespoon rum |
| | 1 cup (8 fl oz, 250 ml) milk |
| 10 cups (4 pints, 2.5 litres) water | ½ teaspoon grated nutmeg |
| sugar | strawberry syrup |

If dried Irish moss is to be used, soak it for a few hours in some water. Otherwise, clean the fresh moss of all other bits of seaweed and wash thoroughly to remove any sand and grit.

Simmer the moss in the water until tender, then top up the water to the original level and bring to the boil. Strain the liquid through a muslin cloth or fine sieve. Add sugar to taste, then add the rum, milk, nutmeg, and enough strawberry syrup to make it pink in colour. Transfer the liquid to a glass bowl and refrigerate until it has set. This jelly has a very delicate and subtle flavour.

Irish moss is also made into a more liquid form and sold as a drink.

## TRIFLE

2¼ cups (¾ pint, 500 ml) fresh
   cream *or* 3 tins cream
4 cups (1½ pints, 1 litre) milk
1 cup (8 oz, 250 g) sugar
6 egg yolks, lightly beaten
1 tablespoon rum
1 teaspoon vanilla

½ teaspoon grated lime rind
1 sponge cake
1 fresh pineapple, *or* 2 cups'
   (20 oz, 575 g) tinned
2 large or 4 small mangoes, sliced,
   *or* 2 cups (20 oz, 575 g) tinned

First make a custard as follows. In a heavy pan heat the cream and milk on a low heat, then add the sugar and the lightly beaten eggs. Keep stirring until it becomes very thick. Do not allow it to boil as it will curdle. Now add the rum, vanilla, and lime rind. Remove the custard from the heat and allow it to cool.

In the meantime line a square dish with half the sponge cake, cut into slices about 1 inch (3 cm) thick. On top of this, pour half the cooled custard, spreading it well over the cake pieces, then add half the fruit. (If you use tinned fruit, drain off the liquid.) Repeat with the remaining ingredients. Refrigerate until required.

## BANANA CUSTARD

⅔ cup (4 oz, 125 g) brown sugar
2 bananas
1 cup (8 oz, 250 g) sugar

1 teaspoon vanilla
6 eggs, well beaten

Melt the brown sugar over a low heat until it turns to a liquid. Quickly pour it to coat the bottom of an ovenproof dish or individual small dishes.

To make the custard, mash the bananas until they are smooth, then add the sugar, vanilla and eggs. Mix well, and pour the mixture into the caramelized dish. Place in a pan of water so that the water comes just about half-way up the dish, and bake at 325°F, 160°C, gas 3, until firm (about 40 minutes for a large dish, 30 minutes for small ones). When done, a thin skewer inserted in the centre will come out clean. Cool, then put in the refrigerator. When you are ready to serve the custard, loosen the edges and turn it out on to a serving dish. Enough for 4.

## SEVILLE ORANGE CUSTARD

rind of ½ Seville orange
juice of 1 Seville orange
1 tablespoon brandy
½ cup (4 oz, 125 g) sugar

4 egg yolks
2½ cups (1 pint, 600 ml) very hot
  milk
honey or brown sugar

Boil the orange rind in a good quantity of water until it is tender, then pound it in a mortar until it is quite fine, or use a blender. Scrape the rind into a bowl, and add the juice, brandy, sugar and the unbeaten egg yolks. Pour in the hot milk and mix well.

Fill individual ovenproof dishes and place them in a container of hot water to come half-way up the dishes. Bake at 325°F, 160°C, gas 3, or simmer on the stove until the custard sets (30–40 minutes). When done, a thin skewer inserted in the centre will come out clean. Decorate the tops with honey or brown sugar, then refrigerate.

## ❋PUDDINGS, PIES, TARTS, BISCUITS

In old Jamaica, and indeed up until not so many years ago, the cast iron or clay coalpot served as a cooker and baker for most households. A slow fire was kept going under the container holding the pudding mixture, and on top was placed a tin sheet of live coals. Both fires were constantly adjusted to maintain an even temperature so that the pudding was not like that described in song: 'de bottom bun (burn) an' de middle raw.'

This method of baking no doubt involved strenuous work, but it certainly produced the most delicious puddings, and to my mind they are not the same baked in our modern gas and electric ovens.

All these puddings are fattening and filling, so I prefer to serve them after a light meal.

## BREAD PUDDING

Bread pudding was probably invented to use up stale bread in the household. Whatever the reason, it became a favourite sweet.

½ lb (250 g) bread
1½ cups (12 fl oz, 350 ml) milk
1 cup (8 fl oz, 250 ml) coconut
  milk (see p. 135)
⅓ cup (2 oz, 50 g) raisins

1 teaspoon vanilla
¼ teaspoon nutmeg
approx. 1 cup (8 oz, 250 g) sugar
2 eggs, beaten

Break the bread into small pieces and place them in a large bowl. Add the milk and coconut milk and leave to soak until the bread is completely saturated. Break up any remaining lumps in the bread and add the raisins, vanilla, nutmeg, and sugar to taste. Finally add the beaten eggs. Pour the mixture immediately into a glass or other ovenproof dish and bake in the oven, preheated to 350°F, 180°C, gas 4, for approximately 45 minutes or until the top is golden brown.

## CASSAVA PONE

2 lb (1 kg) sweet cassava, peeled
  and grated
1 mature coconut, peeled of
  brown skin and grated
1 teaspoon vanilla

½ teaspoon nutmeg
sugar
2 cups (¾ pint, 500 ml) milk
1 cup (8 fl oz, 250 ml) coconut
  milk (see p. 135)

In a large bowl combine the grated cassava and coconut. Mix in the vanilla, nutmeg, and sugar to taste. Add the milk and coconut milk gradually until you have a soft but thick batter; add a little water if necessary. Pour the mixture into a greased baking dish and bake in a moderately hot oven at 350°F, 180°C, gas 4, for 1 hour or until set.

For a rich topping, add 1 cup (8 fl oz, 250 g) of sweetened coconut milk with 2 tablespoons of butter as soon as the pudding starts to set.

## CHRISTMAS PUDDING

Christmas has always had special significance for us, since the days of slavery. It was the most important holiday for the slaves, who received only three days' holiday all year: Christmas Day, Boxing Day and New Year's Day. Relieved of their hard toil, they would shed their ragged oznaburg clothing, and dress themselves in fine clothes and trinkets. On those three days they lived in a world of make-believe; they adopted important English names and a certain amount of licence was allowed them in their relationship with their masters.

Boxing Day was the day for John Canoe or Jonkunoo dancing, part of an elaborate parade through the streets of the town. The dance was of African origin, although the source of its name remains unknown. During the nineteenth century, the centre of attraction at the parade was the procession of the rival Blue and Red set girls, an entirely Jamaican custom. M. G. Lewis describes such a procession in *Journal of a West Indian Proprietor* (1834):

First marched Britannia; then came a band of music; then the flag; then the Blue King and Queen – the Queen splendidly dressed in white and silver (in scorn of the opposite party, her train was borne by a little girl in red); His Majesty wore a full British Admiral's uniform, with a white satin sash, a huge cocked hat with a gilt paper crown on top of it. These were immediately followed by 'Nelson's car', being a kind of canoe decorated with blue and silver drapery and with 'Trafalgar' written on the front of it; and the procession was closed by a long train of blue grandees (the women dressed in uniform of white with robes of blue Muslin), all princes, Dukes and Duchesses, every mother's child of them.

The music that accompanies the Jonkunoo has a peculiar air that cannot be mistaken. It conjured up in me, as a child, a mixture of excitement and fear. We lived then in Spanish Town, on a street which led to the market and hence was a favourite route for the Jonkunoo. They came down the street accompanied by musicians and a crowd of people. Each of them – the Devil, Horsehead, Woman, Actor Boy, Policeman – was masked. I was terrified of the Devil, so at the first sound of the Jonkunoo music I would run into the house, position myself behind half-shuttered jalousies, and view them from this protection.

The Christmas pudding was part of the masters' Christmas fare. Now every year, as Christmas approaches, each household starts the ritual of soaking the fruits for the pudding. It is all part of the excitement of the season. The recipe is still that introduced by the English – and almost all the ingredients called for are imported – but we have added our own rum.

The quantities given should make two 1-quart (1.25-litre) puddings, about 8 × 3 inches (20 × 8 cm).

In a large jar soak the following for at least two weeks:

1 lb (500 g) raisins
½ lb (250 g) currants
½ lb (250 g) stoned prunes
¼ lb (125 g) mixed peel
2 cups (¾ pint, 450 ml) white proof rum *or* other rum
4 cups (1½ pints, 1 litre) port

*Other ingredients*
1⅔ cups (10 oz, 300 g) brown sugar

2 tablespoons water
1½ cups (8 oz, 250 g) flour
1 cup (5 oz, 150 g) breadcrumbs
1 teaspoon baking powder
½ teaspoon salt
1 cup (8 oz, 250 g) butter
6 eggs
½ teaspoon nutmeg
½ teaspoon cinnamon
1 tablespoon vanilla
rind of 1 lime, grated
4 oz (125 g) chopped nuts (optional)

Strain the soaked fruits, reserving the liquid. Mince the fruits, put them in a pan, and add 2 cups (¾ pint, 500 ml) of the liquid in which they were soaked. Simmer for 15 minutes, stirring constantly. Set aside to cool.

In the meantime, heat ⅓ cup (2 oz, 50 g) of the brown sugar with the water until it turns a very dark brown colour, and set aside.

Sieve together the flour, breadcrumbs, baking powder and salt, and set aside.

Cream the butter, gradually adding the rest of the brown sugar and the eggs, one at a time. Mix well after each addition. Add the cooled fruit, melted sugar, nutmeg, cinnamon, vanilla, lime rind and chopped nuts, then stir in the flour mixture.

Choose pudding basins or tins with tight-fitting covers, line them with greaseproof paper, and pour in the mixture to within about 1 inch (2.5 cm) of the top. Place some greased paper on the top of each pudding and cover it.

Use a large pan for steaming the puddings. Place an upturned pie tin in the pan, lower in a pudding and add enough water to reach half-way up the pudding basin or tin. Bring the water to the boil, then simmer, adding hot water as necessary to keep the water level at its original height, until the pudding shrinks from the sides of the basin or tin (about 3 hours).

The Christmas pudding can be served hot or cold with the hard sauce given below.

## BRANDY OR HARD SAUCE

½ cup (4 oz, 125 g) butter  
2 cups (8 oz, 250 g) sifted icing sugar

3 tablespoons brandy

Cream the butter until it is light and fluffy, then add the sifted icing sugar, a little at a time, mixing it in until it is well blended with the butter. Pour in the brandy and mix.

Transfer the sauce to a small serving bowl, and refrigerate until required.

## CORNMEAL PONE

As a child attending the Catholic Elementary School in Spanish Town, the most interesting parts of the day were the recesses. The school gate would disgorge its hundreds of happy children, who rushed to buy snow balls (chopped ice) with brilliantly red syrup poured over them, or Jew plums, guineps, mangoes and whatever fruit was in season. To the other side were the vendors with their show cases of saltfish fritters, cornmeal pone, potato pone, gizadas and cut cakes. I remember being warned by my mother not to buy the cornmeal and potato pones, but whether I heeded her warning remains vague in my memory. I can only remember that this was a child's paradise.

In order to make a good cornmeal pone one has to remember that the cornmeal swells, and if there is insufficient liquid it will be dry and brittle.

2¾ cups (1 lb, 500 g) cornmeal
⅓ cup (2 oz, 50 g) flour
6 cups (2½ pints, 1.5 litres)
  coconut milk (see p. 135)
2⅔ cups (1 lb, 500 g) brown
  sugar
½ teaspoon nutmeg
1 tablespoon vanilla

¼ cup (2 fl oz, 50 ml) rum
1⅓ cups (8 oz, 250 g) raisins

*Topping*
1 cup (8 fl oz, 250 ml) coconut
  milk (see p. 135)
½ cup (3 oz, 90 g) brown sugar
¼ cup (2 oz, 60 g) butter

Put the cornmeal and flour in a bowl and add the coconut milk, a little at a time, mixing well until you have a smooth batter. Then stir in the rest of the ingredients. The mixture should be liquid rather than thick. Pour it into a greased or lined baking tin, and bake in a preheated oven at 300°F, 150°C, gas 2, for approximately 30 minutes, or until the pone starts to set. Pour on the topping ingredients, mixed together, and bake for a further 30 minutes, or until a skewer inserted into the pone comes out clean. Cool before serving.

Cornmeal pone is eaten as a dessert or as a snack.


## CHO CHO PUDDING

3 large cho chos
4 cloves *or* pimento berries
1 cinnamon leaf *or* piece of stick
  cinnamon
1½ cups (6 oz, 175 g)
  breadcrumbs

½ cup (3 oz, 75 g) raisins
1 cup (8 oz, 250 g) sugar
juice of 1 lime
2 eggs, well beaten

Boil the cho chos with the cloves or pimento berries and the cinnamon until tender. Remove the spices and mash the cho chos. Put the mixture in a clean muslin cloth and wring out the excess moisture.

To the cho cho mixture add the breadcrumbs, raisins, sugar and lime juice. Mix well, then add the eggs. Pour the mixture into a buttered pudding dish or tin with a lid, and boil in the same way as Christmas pudding (see p. 147) for 2 hours. It can be eaten hot or cold.

## DOKONO (BLUE DRAWERS)

Here is one recipe which is straight out of Africa. Leonard Barrett, in *The Sun and the Drum* (1976), describes vividly his encounter with this old sweet in the Gold Coast.

As a boy, my Mother often cooked a speciality for us which was always a welcome change in the village menu. She would soak or boil dried corn on the cob, then grate or pound it into flour in a mortar. She would mix the flour with sugar, nutmeg, salt, adding a little wheat flour to thicken it. She then cut the batter into 1 pound pieces, wrapped each in banana leaves, and put them in boiling water for an hour, after which she cooled and served one to each of us. The name of this morsel is 'dokono'. In 1969 on my first trip to Africa, our party stopped at the Koromantyn Market at the foot of the famous Koromantyn Castle from which most Jamaican slaves embarked on their Atlantic journey to Jamaica. Walking in the market, I came upon a woman with a stall of the same banana leaf preparation. I pointed to it and said 'dokono'. The woman, who spoke no English, was startled. She ran and called a man who spoke English and Twi. On their way back to me, the woman was frantically explaining something to him. He finally caught up with me and asked how I knew that the items were dokono. I told him that my mother used to make them and referred to them by that name in Jamaica. In a few minutes I was in the midst of a noisy admiring crowd of old men and women all talking to one another. Some came close, hugging my hands in a most caressing manner. The gentleman explained to me that the elders were giving me an African welcome because I was the son of an ancestor who was sold in slavery. He further explained that the name 'dokono' was a Fanti word which was used only among the people of the Cape Coast and that the knowledge of the name among my family was sufficient evidence that my grandparents came from the region.

Here is the recipe given by Mrs Saul Solomon in *The Peter Pan Book of Recipes* (1929).

'To one pint or half pound of cornmeal mixed with the milk of a coconut and sweetened with new sugar to taste, add a few currants and a little ground cinnamon. Mix it so that it will hold together, and is not too watery, and fold the mixture in quailed banana or plantain leaves, which have been washed and cut in small squares, then tie each one like a small parcel with the trash; put it in a pot and boil. Serve hot.'

(To 'quail' banana leaves, pour some boiling water over the squares and leave them for a few minutes. They will then become pliable and easy to fold. Instead of banana trash, you can use string to tie the parcels.)

## SWEET POTATO PUDDING

2 lb (1 kg) sweet potatoes
1 medium coco
4 cups (1½ pints, 1 litre) coconut milk (see p. 135)
½ cup (3 oz, 75 g) raisins
1 teaspoon vanilla
½ teaspoon nutmeg
sugar

*Topping*
1 cup (8 fl oz, 250 ml) coconut milk (see p. 135)
½ cup (4 oz, 125 g) sugar
a few raisins

Peel and grate the sweet potatoes and coco, and mix in the coconut milk, raisins, vanilla, nutmeg and sugar to taste. The mixture should be runny rather than thick. Pour it into a buttered baking pan or ovenproof dish, and bake in a moderately hot oven – 350°F, 180°C, gas 4, for 1 hour, or until the top becomes solid. Take a fork and scrape the top, and add the topping ingredients mixed together. Bake for a further 30 minutes, or until a skewer inserted into the pudding comes out clean. Cool before serving.

## BASIC PIE PASTRY

½ teaspoon salt
1 cup (5 oz, 150 g) flour

⅓ cup (2½ oz, 75 g) butter
iced water

Sift together the salt and flour, then add the butter and, using a knife, cut it into smaller pieces while combining it with the flour. Pour in some iced water, mixing it in a little at a time, until the pastry holds together but is not sticky. Add a little more flour if necessary. Wrap the pastry in foil and keep it refrigerated until you are ready to use it.

## BANANA TART

8 ripe bananas
5 tablespoons sugar
¼ cup (2 oz, 50 g) butter
½ cup (4 fl oz, 125 ml) water

approx. 2 tablespoons rum
juice of 1 lime
basic pie pastry (see p. 153)

Peel two of the bananas, chop them into small pieces and put them in a small pan. Add the sugar, butter, water and rum. Bring to the boil, then lower the heat and simmer until the mixture thickens. Remove from the heat.

Meanwhile, line a pie tin with the pastry. Peel the rest of the bananas, cut them into rounds, and arrange them in circles so that they overlap and cover the pastry. Sprinkle the lime juice over the bananas, and pour the cooked banana glaze over them. Bake the pie in a preheated oven at 400°F, 200°C, gas 6, for 45 minutes or until brown.

## PINEAPPLE PIE

1 small pineapple
1 cup (8 fl oz, 250 ml) water

1 cup (8 oz, 250 g) sugar
basic pie pastry (see p. 153)

Peel the pineapple and cut it into small slices. Place them in a pan with the water and simmer until they are tender – about 10 minutes. Lift out the pineapple and set aside. Add the sugar to the juice remaining in the pan, and simmer until it thickens and becomes syrupy. Leave to cool.

Meanwhile line a pie tin with the pastry. Arrange the pineapple pieces on the pastry and pour over the cooled syrup. Bake in a preheated oven at 400°F, 200°C, gas 6, for 45 minutes or until brown.

# CHO CHO PIE

4 cho chos
1 cup (8 fl oz, 250 ml) water
6 cloves or pimento berries
1 cup (8 oz, 250 g) sugar

juice of 2 limes
double quantity basic pie pastry
  (see p. 153)
grated rind of 1 lime

Peel and core the cho chos and cut them into small pieces. Simmer them in the water with the cloves or pimento berries until they are tender, then remove the fruit from the pan, discard the cloves or pimento, and set aside. To the juice remaining, add the sugar and lime juice. Simmer this until it becomes thick and syrupy, then set aside to cool.

Line a pie tin with half the pie pastry. Arrange the cho cho pieces on it, sprinkle them with the lime rind and pour the cooled syrup over them. Roll out the remaining pastry and cover the pie. Crimp or seal the edges, and make two slits in the top of the pie to allow the steam to escape. Bake in a preheated oven at 400°F, 200°C, gas 6, for 45 minutes or until brown.

# GUAVA PIE

12 guavas
2 cups (¾ pint, 500 ml) water
1 cup (8 oz, 250 g) sugar

double quantity basic pie pastry
  (see p. 153)

Peel the guavas, cut them in half, and remove the seeds. Cut each half into two pieces. Place the guavas in a pan with the water and sugar, cook them for 10 minutes, then remove the fruit from the pan and set aside. Reduce the remaining liquid by quick boiling until it thickens.

Line a shallow pie tin with half the pastry. Fill it with the guavas, then pour the syrup over them. Cover with the remaining pastry, making two slits in it to allow the steam to escape. Bake in a preheated oven at 400°F, 200°C, gas 6, for 45 minutes or until brown.

## MANGO PIE

This is made in the same way as guava pie, above, with or without the top pastry. Choose meaty but not hairy mangoes. In fact, any other fruit, such as otaheite or rose apples, can make delicious tarts and pies.

## PLANTAIN TARTS

3 very ripe plantains
sugar
nutmeg
vanilla

red food colouring
double quantity basic pie pastry
(see p. 153)

Boil the plantains in water until they are tender (about 15 minutes), then drain and mash them with a fork until they are free of lumps. Add sugar, nutmeg, vanilla and a drop or two of red food colouring.

Roll out the pastry, and cut out 8 circles using a small plate. Place some of the plantain mixture on half of each circle, fold the other half over, and crimp the edges with a fork.

Bake them on ungreased baking sheets at 400°F, 200°C, gas 6, for 30–45 minutes or until golden brown.

## GIZADAS

1 mature coconut, grated
⅔ cup (4 oz, 125 g) brown sugar

½ teaspoon nutmeg
basic pie pastry (see p. 153)

Add the brown sugar and nutmeg to the grated coconut. Pinch off pingpong-sized balls from the pastry, and roll them out into circles. Pinch the edges to form a ridge all the way round, and fill each with the coconut mixture. Bake them at 375°F, 190°C, gas 5, for 20 minutes, or until the pastry is golden and the filling brown.

## BANANA BISCUITS

1 cup (5 oz, 150 g) flour
2 teaspoons baking powder
¼ teaspoon salt
2 very ripe bananas

1 tablespoon (½ oz, 15 g)
  softened butter
2 tablespoons sugar

Sift together the flour, baking powder and salt. Mix in the very well mashed bananas, the butter and the sugar. Add a little more flour if the dough is sticky, then roll it out on a floured board and cut out the desired shapes. Bake the biscuits in a moderately hot oven, 350°F, 180°C, gas 4, for 10–15 minutes. Makes approximately 10–12 biscuits.

## COCONUT BISCUITS

1 dry coconut, grated, dark skin
  removed
½ cup (4 oz, 125 g) sugar
3 tablespoons (1½ oz, 45 g)
  butter

2 eggs, beaten
1½ cups (7 oz, 225 g) flour
3 teaspoons baking powder
½ teaspoon salt

Combine the grated coconut, sugar and butter, mixing them well together. Stir in the beaten eggs. Sift the flour with the baking powder and salt, and add. The batter must not be runny, but should be a very thick paste that will not spread too much. Drop spoonfuls of the mixture on to a greased baking sheet and bake in a moderately hot oven at 350°F, 180°C, gas 4, until brown. The biscuits will keep fresh for several weeks in an airtight tin.

## COCONUT MACAROONS

This is a good recipe for using up egg whites.

4 egg whites, beaten
2 cups (8 oz, 250 g) icing sugar
1 teaspoon vanilla

½ cup (2½ oz, 60 g) flour
2 cups (8 oz, 250 g) grated
  coconut, dark skin removed

Beat the egg whites until they are very stiff and form peaks. Gradually add the icing sugar and vanilla, beating the mixture well after each addition. Then fold in the sifted flour, and lastly add the grated coconut.

Drop spoonfuls of the mixture on to a greased baking sheet and bake in a moderately hot oven, 350°F, 180°C, gas 4, for 30 minutes or until brown. Makes approximately 24 macaroons.

## #WATER ICES

Fruit ices, Italian ices and granitas are not popular in Jamaica for some reason, although commercially produced ice cream has flourished over the years. We do make frozen icicles from fruit juices, but the result is a solid mass of ice.

The secret of making good water ices at home is first to make a syrup base and then to add fresh fruit juice. After the mixture has been in the freezer for 1 hour, it must be beaten with a whisk or fork in order to break up the large ice crystals. If this is repeated twice more, at 30-minute intervals, the resulting granita or ice will be very smooth and fluffy, with tiny ice granules instead of the hard mass we are accustomed to.

## BASIC SYRUP FOR WATER ICES

4 cups (1½ pints, 1 litre) water        2 cups (1 lb, 500 g) sugar

Boil the water and sugar together for 10 minutes, then cool.

Add to this syrup an equal quantity of either a fruit purée or a juice. Mix well and transfer to the freezer in a suitable container. To freeze, turn the freezer to its coldest temperature. After 1 hour beat the ice with a fork to break up the crystals that have formed; repeat this two or three times more at 30-minute intervals.

FRUIT SUITABLE FOR PURÉES
   Mangoes, star apples, pawpaw, strawberries, guavas, naseberries.

FRUIT JUICES
   Any juice will do, but the stronger the flavour the better the ice will
   be. Try lemon, lime, pineapple, tangerine, garden cherry, mango,
   grapefruit, tamarind, pomegranate, ortanique.

## WATER COCONUT ICE

To the basic water ice recipe above, add the coconut water taken
from 2 or more young water coconuts; add the soft jelly to the
water as well. Freeze as directed in the basic recipe.

## ✳ICE CREAM

We have a long list of fruit suitable for making ice cream, yet the
commercial manufacturers, with few exceptions, continue to
produce artificially scented ice cream such as peach and cherry. It
is obviously much cheaper to produce ice cream without fruit, and
less of a bother to continue to make it from recipes that come with
the machines.

   Good ice cream is expensive and a luxury, originally made from
fresh cream, fruit and sugar with very little else needed in the way
of thickening. However, ice cream differs from country to
country, according to the ingredients available. We have no fresh
cream in Jamaica, so we usually have to resort to using tinned
cream, evaporated milk or plain milk. I have, however, worked
out a recipe for a good custard using milk and more eggs. If you
are lucky enough to come by some cream, then fewer eggs can be
used. To this custard you can add any fruit purée to make a very
good ice cream.

## BASIC CUSTARD FOR ICE CREAM

1 ½ cups (12 oz, 350 g) sugar          1 teaspoon vanilla
8 egg yolks
4 cups (1 ½ pints, 1 litre) milk,
   boiled

Place the sugar and egg yolks in a saucepan. Work the mixture with a wooden spoon until it begins to thicken and reach a ribbony consistency, that is, until it will fall slowly from the spoon. Add the very hot milk, little by little. Add the vanilla and transfer the pan to a low heat. Keep stirring constantly until the custard sticks to the spoon. It should be neither very thick nor too liquid. It must not be allowed to come to the boil, or it will curdle. Rub the custard through a fine sieve and leave it to cool. (This is the basic custard used in the recipes that follow.)

Add 2 cups (¾ pint, 500 ml) of the fruit purée of your choice, and transfer the mixture to the refrigerator to cool before freezing. (This makes the freezing process much quicker.)

This amount is enough for a 3-quart (3-litre) ice cream maker.

If the ice cream is to be made in an electric or hand-cranked bucket, follow the instructions given by the manufacturers. Remember that you must leave some space for the ice cream to expand, so fill the container about three-quarters full.

If the ice cream is to be made in the freezer, transfer it to aluminium trays if possible. After it has been in the freezer for 1 hour, beat it vigorously with a fork or whisk to break up the large ice crystals. Repeat this process 2–3 times at 30-minute intervals. The texture of ice cream made in the freezer will not be as smooth as that produced by the ice cream maker. Nevertheless, it will be delicious.

## BANANA ICE CREAM

Purée or mash 6 very ripe bananas to a smooth consistency, and add to the cooled basic custard. Freeze as directed.

## COCONUT ICE CREAM

Grate a large mature coconut and pour on 2 cups (¾ pint, 500 ml) of warm water. Mix thoroughly with your hands and squeeze the coconut to get out as much of the milk as possible. Pour through a very fine sieve, squeezing out all the juice from the grated coconut, or pour through a muslin cloth and squeeze the muslin to extract the rest of the liquid. Add this coconut milk to the cooled basic custard, and freeze as directed.

## GUAVA ICE CREAM

Peel and halve 12 ripe guavas and steam them in very little water until they are tender. Rub them through a sieve, leave to cool, then add to the cooled basic custard and freeze as directed.

## MANGO ICE CREAM

Make 1 cup (½ pint, 250 ml) of mango purée by rubbing some mangoes through a sieve. Use Bombays if you can get them, for they make a very fine ice cream, but any other mango will do. Add the purée to the cooked basic custard and freeze as directed.

## PINEAPPLE ICE CREAM

Add 2 cups (1½ lb, 750 g) of freshly grated or shredded pineapple to the cooled basic custard and freeze as directed.

## SOURSOP ICE CREAM

Remove the skin and inner core of a small soursop. Add 2 cups (¾ pint, 500 ml) of water to the pulp and mix it very well with your fingers or a spoon to extract the juice from the fruit. Strain through a sieve, pressing out as much of the juice as you can. Add this juice to the cooled basic custard, and freeze as directed.

This is a delicious and distinctive ice cream.

# RUM DRINKS, LIQUEURS, WINES AND FRUIT DRINKS

# ✳ RUM DRINKS

The history of rum is a long one. The origin of its name is uncertain, but perhaps the most likely explanation lies in the botanical name of sugar, *Saccharum officinarum*, which, it is said, was shortened to 'rum'.

Jamaican rum was the first to be commercially produced by the distillation process, introduced by the British shortly after their conquest of the island in 1655. For a very long time in the West Indies rum was considered the drink of sailors and persons of low status. The literature and historical documents spanning the period up to the nineteenth century suggest very strongly that the average white person drank only imported liquor. Rum appears in European literature, however, as something very exotic and mysterious. With the advent of cocktails in the 1920s, rum became very popular.

Our rum, ranging from pale amber to dark gold, enjoys a high reputation with connoisseurs world-wide. The rum drunk in Jamaica is subtler in flavour than those generally available in the U.K., which are imported in bulk and then blended.

Rum is made from molasses, a by-product of sugar. Its production has three stages: fermentation, distillation and ageing. At the fermentation stage, water and yeast are added to the molasses, and chemical and biochemical changes occur which break down the sugar into alcohol. The extraction of the rum is done by distillation, using the pot still or the more modern continuous still. At this stage the rum is colourless.

The traditional ageing process required that the rum be stored in oak casks for a period of between three and twenty years, depending on the type of rum and the bouquet required. Oak casks produce a light amber-coloured rum; darker rums are coloured with caramel. The use of oak casks is, however, declining, and rum is now often stored in vats at the supplier stage. It is left to mature for between one and three years. Caramel is used to colour this rum.

The white through to dark rums contain approximately 40–

46% alcohol by volume. The relatively rare twenty-year-old rum is comparable with a very good cognac.

White overproof or 'proof' rum contains 57–63% alcohol, with the proof stage defined as 57% alcohol. Because of its high alcohol content, overproof rum is not available in Britain, as laws specify a maximum of 46% alcohol by volume.

White proof rum holds an interesting position in our households. People swear by it for its medicinal properties. Mainly used as a rub, it is also poured on the 'mole', the top of the head, during fevers and to prevent colds. I have also found that it provides immediate relief for hay fever when inhaled.

White rum plays an important part in our folk culture. An addition to a house calls for the sprinkling of a little white rum over the area to be enclosed, and a new house should not be occupied unless white rum has been sprinkled at the four corners to ward off 'spirits' or the evil eye.

### ✱PROVERBS✱

Beware a rum seller as a story teller.

Rum shop no de place fe find good spirit.

When de rum a in, de wit a out.

Dem dat always drinkin' always dry.

## BANANA DAIQUIRI

3 tablespoons light rum
1 tablespoon sugar
2 tablespoons lime juice

a few slices banana
crushed ice

Mix the rum, sugar, lime juice and banana in a blender, or crush the bananas and add to the other ingredients. Mix well and serve on crushed ice. Enough for 1.

## COCONUT DAIQUIRI

3 tablespoons coconut cream (see p. 142)
4 tablespoons white proof rum

2 tablespoons lime juice
crushed ice

Mix the coconut cream, rum and lime juice well and serve on crushed ice. Enough for 1.

## JAMAICA PLANTERS' PUNCH

4 tablespoons white sugar
1 tablespoon lime juice
4 tablespoons water
8 tablespoons light rum

2 slices pineapple, peeled
crushed ice
2 cherries

Combine the sugar, lime juice, water and rum, and mix well until the sugar is dissolved. Chop the pineapple into small pieces and add these to the liquid. Mix well and serve on crushed ice, decorated with a cherry. Enough for 2.

## PRICKLY PEAR PUNCH

The prickly pear, more commonly called tuna, is a member of the cactus family. The fruit is about 3 inches (7 cm) long and prickly all over, and the flesh underneath is bright red. It makes a very beautiful punch.

2 cups (¾ pint, 500 ml) prickly pear juice
1 cup (8 fl oz, 250 ml) rum

sugar
crushed ice

Mix the prickly pear juice and rum together. Sweeten with a little sugar if necessary and serve on crushed ice. Enough for 4.

## RUM COLLINS

| | |
|---|---|
| 2 tablespoons lime juice | crushed ice |
| 2 tablespoons sugar | soda water |
| 4 tablespoons rum | a few slices of lime *or* 1 cherry |

Mix together the lime juice, sugar and rum and stir until the sugar is dissolved. Pour the mixture over crushed ice and add some soda water. Decorate with slices of lime or a cherry. Enough for 1.

## RUM MINT JULEP

| | |
|---|---|
| 2 sprigs mint | crushed ice |
| 1 tablespoon sugar | 4 tablespoons rum |
| 4 tablespoons water | |

Place 1 sprig of mint and the sugar in a glass, add the water, and mix well until the sugar dissolves. Remove the mint, put some crushed ice in the glass and add the rum. Mix well and decorate with the remaining sprig of mint. Enough for 1.

## JAMAICA RUM PUNCH

During the eighteenth century the Caribbean was notorious for its pirates. Among the most terrifying of them all was Jack Rackham or 'Calico Jack', so called because of his fondness for calico underclothes. But the Governor of Jamaica, Sir Nicholas Laws, was determined to get rid of him, as he frequented the Jamaican shores.

Laws heard in November 1720 that Calico Jack was in Ocho Rios, and he dispatched a Captain Barnet to apprehend him. Calico Jack was finally found in Negril Bay enjoying a rum punch party, and was captured. It was then discovered that two of his notorious crew members were women – Anne Bonney and Mary Read.

Calico Jack was executed. His body was put in an iron frame and hung on a cay off Port Royal – still known today as Rackham's Cay – as a warning to other pirates.

This is the basic recipe for our famous rum punch.

| | |
|---|---|
| 1 part sour | – lime juice |
| 2 parts sweet | – sugar, syrup |
| 3 parts strong | – rum |
| 4 parts weak | – water or any fruit juice |

Mix the ingredients well and serve on crushed ice, decorated with pieces of sliced pineapple, lime or lemon.


# ✷LIQUEURS

## FALARIUM

This is an old recipe whose source I have been unable to find.

2 cups (¾ pint, 500 ml) lime juice     8 cups (3 pints, 2 litres) water
6 cups (2¼ pints, 1.5 litres) white     5 cups (2½ lb, 1.25 kg) sugar
    proof rum     juice of 3 oranges

Add the lime juice to the rum, then mix in the other ingredients. Store in a cask or bottles to mature for a month. Makes approximately 8 pints (4.5 litres).


## PINEAPPLE LIQUEUR

4 cups (1½ pints, 1 litre) white     2 cups (¾ pint, 500 ml) lime juice
    proof rum     4½ cups (2¼ lb, 1.1 kg) sugar
1 whole pineapple, peeled and
    chopped

Mix all the ingredients together in a large bowl. Cover and leave for 2 days, then strain through a muslin cloth into sterilized bottles. Allow to mature for a month. Makes approximately 4 pints (2.5 litres).

## PIMENTO DRAM

4–5 cups (1½–2 pints, 1–1.25 litres) ripe pimento berries

5 cups (1 pint, 1.25 litres) white proof rum

2½ cups (2 pints, 600 ml) lime juice

10 cups (4 pints, 2.5 litres) water

2 cups (1¼ lb, 600 g) sugar

4 oz (125 g) cinnamon sticks

Wash the pimento berries and place them in a large glass or earthenware container. Pour the rum over them, then the lime juice, and leave for a week.

Make a syrup with the water and sugar, adding the cinnamon. Strain the pimento liquid through a muslin cloth, taking care not to crush the berries. Discard the berries (or put them to dry in the sun – you can then use these in the usual manner). Add the cooled syrup to the strained liquid. Mix well, then strain through some clean muslin.

Store the liqueur in sterilized bottles, preferably in a dark cupboard, to mature for a month. A certain amount of sediment will form at the bottom. If you wish to get rid of it, pour off as much as you can of the top portion, taking care not to shake the bottle or disturb the sediment. Pour into clean bottles again for storage.

The pimento makes an unusual and delicious nectar of a liqueur. Makes approximately 8 pints (4.5 litres).

## SANGAREE

1 cup (8 fl oz, 250 ml) sherry

2 cups (¾ pint, 500 ml) water

½ teaspoon grated nutmeg

sugar

peel of 1 lime

Mix all the ingredients together, and serve over crushed ice. Enough for 4.

## ESSENCE OF GINGER

3 oz (75 g) freshly grated ginger
2 oz (50 g) thinly cut lime peel

5 cups (2 pints, 1.25 litres) white
  proof rum

Mix all the ingredients together in a bowl. Cover, and leave undisturbed for 2 weeks. Strain the liquid through a muslin cloth and store in sterilized bottles.

## ✳ WINES

### GINGER WINE

Caroline Sullivan's recipe for ginger wine, from her *Jamaica Cookery Book* (1893), suggests the tempo and ways of a bygone day.

'20 gallon cask
6 lbs of ginger
11 gallons of water
50 lbs of sugar

5 gallons of rum
5 gallons of lime juice
eggs

Bruise and boil the ginger in the water for 2 hours. You should have about 10 gallons of water then. Dissolve the sugar in this and strain it into the cask; add 5 gallons of 19 percent proof rum and the lime juice. Stir every morning for 3 weeks, then add the whites and shells of 4 eggs to clarify the mixture. The wine should be ready in three weeks.'

## ORANGE WINE

This is another of Caroline Sullivan's recipes, which I have modified.

20 cups (8 pints, 4.75 litres)
orange juice

5 cups (2 pints, 1.25 litres) lime
juice

12 cups (4½ lb, 2.25 kg) brown
sugar

12 cups (5 pints, 3 litres) proof
rum

whites and shells of 2 eggs

1¼ cups (½ pint, 300 ml) fresh
milk

Mix the first four ingredients together in a large jar. Cover, and leave for 3 days. Then add the egg whites and shells, mixed with the milk, to clear the wine. Stir well, and leave for a further 3 days. Strain the mixture through a muslin cloth into clean bottles. It should be ready for use in a month's time. Makes approximately 16 pints (9 litres).

## GRAPEFRUIT WINE

8 grapefruit, peeled and sliced

rind of 1 grapefruit

6 cups (3 lb, 1.5 kg) sugar

1 stick cinnamon

2 whole cloves

1 cup (8 oz, 250 g) raisins

3 cups (1¼ pints, 750 ml) proof
rum

15 cups (6 pints, 3.6 litres) water

Mix all the ingredients together in a large jar. Cover, and leave to mature for 4 weeks. Then strain the mixture through a muslin cloth, preferably into dark bottles, and store them in a dark cupboard. Makes approximately 6 pints (3.5 litres).

## CASHEW WINE

During the summer months, when cashew fruits are plentiful, this is a wonderful way to make use of them. After removing the seeds, prick the fruit all over with a sharp instrument and squeeze out the juice. Use the squeezed fruit to make delicious preserves (see p. 207).

10 cups (4 pints, 2.5 litres) cashew
    juice
6½ cups (3¼ lb, 1.6 kg) brown
    sugar

2 teaspoons grated nutmeg
2½ cups (1 pint, 600 ml) white
    proof rum
2½ cups (1 pint, 600 ml) milk

Mix all the ingredients together in a large jar. Cover and leave
undisturbed for 4 weeks, then strain the liquid into bottles and
store in a dark cupboard. Makes 6 pints (3.5 litres).

## BANANA WINE

12 very ripe bananas
1 cup (7 oz, 200 g) rice
25 cups (10 pints, 5.75 litres)
    water

¼ cup (2 fl oz, 50 ml) liquid tea
9 cups (4½ lb, 2.25 kg) sugar

Slice the bananas, keeping the skins on. Simmer the rice and
bananas in the water for 20 minutes, then add the tea and sugar
and simmer for a further 5 minutes. Cool the mixture, pour into
an earthenware jar, and cover. Leave it for a month, then strain
through a muslin cloth into clean bottles and leave to mature for
another month. Makes 10 pints (5.7 litres).

## ✱ FRUIT DRINKS

For people living in the tropics, cooling drinks are a necessity. We
are blessed with an abundance of fresh fruits, some available all
the year round, others seasonal. Limes, lemons, soursops, pineapples, oranges, grapefruits, tamarinds, mangoes, guavas, garden
cherries – all these make delicious, cooling drinks, and are full of
vitamins.

However, apart from the occasional juice vendor who plies his
trade in the busy sections of Kingston, selling canes, oranges,
soursop juices and Irish moss, and the coconut man, his cart piled
high with young water coconuts, there are few establishments in
Jamaica that sell fresh fruit juice. Yet such places abound in other
West Indian cities. Advertising is probably to blame for the higher

status given to bottled aerated water, which in most cases consists of little more than sugar, water, artificial flavourings and bubbles.

## BANANA MILKSHAKE

4 ripe bananas
½ cup (4 oz, 100 g) sugar

4 cups (1½ pints, 1 litre) milk
½ pint (300 ml) vanilla ice cream

Either crush the bananas very well with a fork, adding the sugar and milk and finally the ice cream, or whisk the ingredients in a blender for a few minutes. Enough for 4.

## BANANA PUNCH

4 ripe bananas
1 cup (8 oz, 250 g) sugar
1½ cups (12 fl oz, 350 ml) water

¼ teaspoon grated nutmeg
1 teaspoon vanilla

Either whisk all the ingredients in a blender, or crush the bananas very well with a fork, add the other ingredients and mix well. Serve on crushed ice. Enough for 2.

## BANANA FRUIT PUNCH

1 small pineapple
3 ripe bananas, crushed
3 cups (1¼ pints, 750 ml) orange
   juice

1 cup (8 fl oz, 250 ml) lime juice
4 cups (1½ pints, 1 litre) water
1 cup (8 oz, 250 g) sugar
½ teaspoon grated nutmeg

Peel and grate the pineapple and add it to the crushed bananas. Add the orange and lime juices, water, sugar and nutmeg. Mix together by hand or whisk in a blender. Serve over crushed ice. Enough for 10.

# BANANA NECTAR

6 ripe bananas                          juice of 3 limes
sugar to taste

Crush the bananas with a fork and beat until smooth, then add the sugar and lime juice. Alternatively, whisk all the ingredients in a blender. Serve on crushed ice. Enough for 3.

## CASHEW PUNCH

This recipe was given to me some years ago by the late Mrs Marie Fox, the mother of Louis Fox, formerly Judge of the Court of Appeal.

'Cashews to be stewed are usually pricked all over and the juice is squeezed out. To 3 cups (1¼ pints, 750 ml) of the juice add the juice of 3 limes and 1 orange. Sweeten to your own taste and serve on crushed ice.'

## CARROT PUNCH

5 large carrots, grated                 5 tablespoons lime juice
4 cups (1½ pints, 1 litre) water        sugar

Grate the carrots, add the water, mix well, then squeeze through a strainer. Add the lime juice and sugar to taste. Mix well and serve on crushed ice. Enough for 4.

The mixture of carrot juice and stout has recently become known as 'culture juice'.

## COCONUT DRINK

Young water coconuts are usually sold from heavily laden mule- or donkey-drawn carts, often positioned in some shady spot by the side of the road where thirsty buyers can enjoy the cool, sweet coconut water in comfort. The vendor expertly slashes off the top of the coconut for the buyer, leaving a small opening at one end from which the water is drunk. Sometimes the coconut contains soft jelly, so the vendor will cut the coconut into two pieces with one slash of his machete. He cuts from the side of the fruit a small piece which one uses as a spoon to scrape out the jelly. This is the best way to enjoy water coconuts.

The following drink is made from the flesh of the mature coconut, which is much firmer than the jelly found in the young fruit.

| | |
|---|---|
| 1 mature coconut | ½ cup (4 oz, 100 g) sugar |
| 3 cups (1¼ pints, 750 ml) water | 1 teaspoon essence of almond |

Break the coconut, reserving the water. Grate the flesh and add to the water. Mix well, strain through a sieve, and to the resulting coconut liquid add the reserved coconut water and the remaining ingredients. Serve on crushed ice. Enough for 3.

## CHERRY CUP

The garden cherry (*M. puniciflora*), known also as acerola, Barbados cherry or West Indian cherry, is native to the West Indies and has been introduced into tropical Asia and Africa. It contains a very high percentage of Vitamin C, much higher than that found in citrus fruit. The juice is extraordinarily delicious.

| | |
|---|---|
| 3 cups (1¼ pints, 750 ml) garden cherries | 1½ cups (12 fl oz, 350 ml) water sugar |

Wash the cherries and add to the water. Rub through a sieve, or whisk in a blender for a few minutes and strain. Sweeten to taste and serve on crushed ice. Serves approximately 3.

## LIME SQUASH

| | |
|---|---|
| juice of 2 limes | soda water |
| sugar | |

Mix the lime juice with the sugar, then add soda water. Stir well and serve on ice.

# GINGER BEER

Ginger beer is one of those delicious brews which has a long history. It is a home-brewed drink, often sold in the markets and now to be found in some fruit and vegetable shops. It is very easy to make, with no special mystique attached to it.

The chewstick used in this recipe is from a climbing vine (*Gouania lupuloides*) found in thickets and woodlands. The sticks are tied in bundles and sold in the markets. Chewstick is often used by people living in country districts to clean their teeth. The stick, which is quite bitter in taste, is first chewed to produce a lather and then the fibrous chewed part is used to rub the gums and teeth. A toothpaste has been developed from the vine. Chewstick is used in certain drinks, as here, to give flavour or body.

2 cups (12 oz, 350 g) grated ginger  
2 3-inch (8-cm) pieces chewstick, chopped small  
20 cups (8 pints, 4.75 litres) water  
1 tablespoon dried yeast  
juice of 6 limes  
approximately 5 cups (2½ lb, 1.25 kg) sugar

Put all the ingredients in a large yabba or earthenware jar, and place in the sun for a day. Strain, bottle and refrigerate. The ginger beer will keep for a week if refrigerated, otherwise for up to 3 days. Makes approximately 8 pints (4.5 litres).


# GUAVA DRINK

ripe guavas  
water  
sugar  
grated nutmeg

Crush the guavas and put them through a sieve. To this purée add water, sugar to taste and a little nutmeg. Serve on crushed ice.

This is a beautiful drink. Those living in countries where the fresh fruit are not available could make it with tinned guavas, using the syrup or juice in the tin in place of some of the sugar and water.

## FRUIT PUNCH

2½ cups (1 pint, 600 ml) orange
   juice
1 cup (8 fl oz, 250 ml) pineapple
   juice
juice of 3 limes

3 cups (1¼ pints, 750 ml) water
½ teaspoon grated nutmeg
½ cup (4 oz, 100 g) sugar
lime or pineapple slices for
   decoration

Combine all the ingredients and mix well. Serve on crushed ice, decorated with lime slices or pieces of pineapple. Enough for 4.

## LEMONADE

Lemonade is perhaps the most popular non-alcoholic drink. Strictly speaking this recipe should be called limeade. However, as limes are more abundant than lemons, 'lemonade' is usually made with limes. Lemons can be substituted. It is usually made with brown sugar, but white sugar also makes good lemonade.

6 cups (2½ pints, 1.5 litres) water
1 cup (8 fl oz, 250 ml) lime juice
   (approximately 12 limes)

1½ cups (11 oz, 340 g) sugar

Pour the water into a jug and add the lime juice and sugar. Mix well until the sugar is dissolved. Serve very cold or on ice.

## MANGO PUNCH

12 ripe mangoes
15 cups (6 pints, 4 litres) water

juice of 2 limes
2 cups (1 lb, 500 g) sugar

Peel the mangoes, remove all the flesh from the stones, and rub through a sieve. To the resulting purée add the water, lime juice and sugar. Mix well, and serve chilled or on crushed ice. Enough for 8.

## OTAHEITE APPLE DRINK

12 otaheite apples, chopped
2 tablespoons grated ginger

5 cups (2 pints, 1.25 litres) water
sugar

Put the apples and ginger in a pan, and add the water. Bring to the boil, then reduce the heat and simmer for 15 minutes or until the apples are cooked. Add enough sugar to sweeten, and stir until dissolved. Remove from the heat and leave to cool.

Strain and serve over crushed ice. Enough for 8.

## PINE DRINK

One of our most delicious and refreshing drinks is made from the peel and discarded pieces of a fresh pineapple.

skin and remains of 1 freshly
  peeled pineapple
1 piece ginger, grated

5 cups (2 pints, 1.25 litres) boiling
  water
sugar

Put the pineapple pieces and skin with the grated ginger in a large container. Add the boiling water and leave overnight. Strain, add sugar to taste, then refrigerate. Serve chilled or on crushed ice. Makes approximately 2 pints (1 litre).

## PLANTAIN DRINK

This is an old recipe, created perhaps at a time when plantains were more abundant than they are today.

Gather the fruit when quite ripe. Pull off the skins, mash the flesh and pour on some boiling water. Let the mixture stand for a night, then strain and bottle the liquid. In a week it will be ready to drink. It is a very pleasant drink and fairly alcoholic.

## PAWPAW DRINK

The pawpaw (*C. papaya L.*) is a native of the tropical Americas.

| | |
|---|---|
| 1 small pawpaw, peeled and sliced | 4 cups (1½ pints, 1 litre) water |
| ½ cup (¼ pint, 150 ml) lime juice | ¾ cup (6 oz, 175 g) sugar |

Crush the pawpaw, add the lime juice, water and sugar, and mix well. Alternatively, combine all the ingredients in a blender. Serve on crushed ice. Enough for 6.

## SORREL

The Jamaica sorrel (*Hibiscus sabdariffa*) is also known as roselle in the Eastern Caribbean. It is a member of the Hibiscus family and native to tropical Asia. From the red, acid petals are made jams, drinks, wine, and a jelly not unlike cranberry. It is an important ingredient in Indian and South East Asian curries and chutneys. It is not related to the European sorrel of the Rumex family, the spinach-like leaves of which are somewhat bitter and sour and are prepared more or less like spinach.

Sorrel is our favourite drink for Christmas and New Year. To my mind it should not be made thick and sweet, for then it becomes sickly and cloying. It should be a light, refreshing drink that one accepts gladly during one's round of Christmas visits, and not one to be avoided.

The drink can be made from dried sorrel or sorrel syrup.

| | |
|---|---|
| 8 cups (3½ pints, 2 litres) sorrel petals | rum |
| | sugar |
| 2 oz (50 g) grated ginger | |
| 12 cups (5 pints, 3 litres) boiling water | |

Place the sorrel and ginger in a large container and pour on the boiling water. Cover and leave overnight, then strain through a muslin cloth or a sieve. Add a little rum to preserve and sugar to sweeten. Bottle and refrigerate. Makes approximately 4½ pints (2.75 litres).

# TAMARIND DRINK

The tamarind (*Tamarindus indice*) is probably native to tropical East Africa or South Asia. It was introduced into Jamaica by the Spaniards during the seventeenth century. From the brown pulp surrounding the seeds is made this popular drink.

| | |
|---|---|
| 4 cups (1½ pints, 1 litre) tamarinds, shelled | 8 cups (3½ pints, 2 litres) water sugar |

Soak the shelled tamarinds in the water overnight, then mash them to remove the pulp. Strain the liquid through a sieve, and add sugar to taste. Refrigerate and serve with ice. Add more water if it is too thick, and adjust the sweetness. Enough for 8.

# SOURSOP DRINK

This is a delicious drink, made from the highly perfumed, somewhat tart flesh of the soursop.

| | |
|---|---|
| 1 medium sized soursop | grated nutmeg |
| 8 cups (3½ pints, 2 litres) water | juice of 1 lime |
| sugar | |

Remove the outer skin and core of the soursop. Add the flesh to the water and mix well, then squeeze through a muslin cloth or sieve. Add sugar to taste, and the grated nutmeg. Refrigerate and serve on ice. Enough for 6.

# SOURSOP PUNCH

| | |
|---|---|
| 2 medium soursops | grated nutmeg |
| 4 cups (1½ pints, 1 litre) water | sugar |
| 4 cups (1½ pints, 1 litre) milk | |

Prepare the soursops as in the previous recipe. Add the water, then to the strained liquid add the milk, grated nutmeg and sugar to sweeten. Enough for 3.

## EGG NOG

In my family, egg nogs were very often served during illness or convalescence, sometimes between breakfast and lunch.

3 eggs  
1 cup (8 oz, 250 g) sugar  
1½ cups (12 fl oz, 350 ml) milk  

4 tablespoons rum  
½ teaspoon grated nutmeg  
1 tablespoon vanilla  

Beat the eggs until they are thick and lemon-coloured, then gradually add the sugar, milk, rum, nutmeg and vanilla. Serve immediately on crushed ice. Enough for 2.

# PORRIDGES

Our porridges are usually breakfast fare, eaten with much gusto and delight. They were doubtless introduced by the British, but ours differ from the true Scottish porridge, which is seasoned only with salt, in that local ingredients are used and are heavily scented or spiced and sweetened. We have transformed the basic porridge to suit our own tastes and disposition.

## BANANA PORRIDGE

4 cups (1½ pints, 1 litre) water
1 cup (8 fl oz, 250 ml) coconut
   milk (see p. 135)
3 green bananas, grated
½ teaspoon nutmeg

1 teaspoon vanilla
½ teaspoon salt
2 tablespoons flour
1 cup (8 fl oz, 250 ml) milk
sugar

Add the water and coconut milk to the peeled, grated bananas and beat the mixture well until it is free of lumps. Bring it to the boil, then lower the heat and simmer for 15 minutes, by which time the bananas should be cooked.

Add the nutmeg, vanilla and salt, and the flour mixed first with a little water. Pour in the milk and add sugar to taste. Continue to simmer, stirring well, until the porridge thickens to the desired consistency. Serve it in bowls, sprinkled with brown sugar or with honey poured over. Enough for 4.

## CASSAVA PORRIDGE

1 lb (500 g) sweet cassava
3 cups (1¼ pints, 750 ml) milk
¼ teaspoon grated nutmeg

½ teaspoon vanilla
sugar

Peel and grate the sweet cassava, then squeeze out most of the juice and discard it. Place the cassava 'bran' in the sun to dry for a day or more, or dry it in a slow oven.

Bring the milk to the boil. Immediately remove the pan from the heat and sprinkle in a cup of the dried cassava, mixing well. Return the pan to the heat and cook over a medium heat for 15 minutes, stirring constantly until the porridge is cooked. Add the nutmeg, vanilla and sugar to taste.

Serve sprinkled with brown sugar, which makes a lovely pattern as it melts.

## CORNMEAL PORRIDGE

1 cup (6 oz, 175 g) cornmeal
4 cups (1½ pints, 1 litre) milk
¼ teaspoon nutmeg
½ teaspoon vanilla

1 cinnamon leaf or ¼ teaspoon ground cinnamon or a small piece of cinnamon stick
sugar

Pour the milk into a pan, add the cornmeal, mix very well to remove lumps, and bring to the boil, stirring constantly. Immediately lower the heat and stir in the nutmeg, vanilla, cinnamon and sugar to taste. Simmer for a further 10 minutes, by which time it should be done. Add extra milk if it should get too thick.

Serve the porridge in bowls and sprinkle some brown sugar on top. A little milk can be poured on top as well.

## HOMINY

One can now buy hominy corn ready prepared. In the past the processing was done at home. The corn was soaked in water and then lightly pounded in a mortar to remove the outer skin. This recipe uses the prepared corn.

2 cups (¾ pint, 500 ml) hominy corn
water
1 cup (8 fl oz, 250 ml) milk
1 cup (8 fl oz, 250 ml) coconut milk (see p. 135)

½ teaspoon ground cinnamon or 1 cinnamon leaf
½ teaspoon nutmeg
sugar

Put the hominy corn to boil with enough water to cover it

completely and bring to the boil. Reduce the heat and continue to
boil until the hominy corn is tender. Then add the milk, coconut
milk, cinnamon, nutmeg and enough sugar to sweeten. Continue
to boil until the liquid is reduced and thickens.

Serve it in bowls, with some brown sugar sprinkled on top of
each. Enough for 4.

# JAMS, JELLIES
# AND MARMALADES

# *HINTS FOR MAKING GOOD JAMS, JELLIES AND MARMALADES

1. Use mature (but not too ripe) fruit, as these have the most pectin, which helps the jam to set. Add lime or lemon juice to those fruits which are low in pectin.
2. It is difficult to control the quality if a large amount of fruit is dealt with in one go, so do not try to make too much at a time.
3. Judge the amount of sugar according to the sweetness of the fruit. Too much sugar will detract from the flavour of the fruit and will make the jam or jelly crystallize, but insufficient sugar might lead to fermentation. Very watery fruits such as watermelon need quite a lot of sugar.
4. It is important to skim the mixture in the early stages of boiling, so as to get rid of froth and any impurities that float to the top.
5. As soon as the mixture starts to form a mass of tiny bubbles, this is a sure sign that the jam or jelly is nearly ready. Test it by dropping a little of it into a saucer of very cold water. If it forms little balls then it is done. You can also test by using a sugar thermometer: the jam or jelly should reach 220°F, 104°C.
6. Be sure to sterilize the jars, either by boiling or by heating them slowly in the oven. This will ensure that fungi will not start growing on top of the jam or jelly.

## SEVILLE ORANGE MARMALADE

3 Seville oranges sugar
6 cups (2½ pints, 1.5 litres) water

Wash the oranges and cut into quarters. Separate the flesh from the skin and cut away the tough core. Remove the seeds, put them in a glass with a little water, and set aside. Mince the rind or cut it into very thin strips. Place the rind and flesh in a large pan and pour in the water. Leave everything to soak overnight.

The following day, put the pan to boil until the rind is tender.

Measure the boiled mixture and for every cup (8 fl oz, 250 ml) add 1 cup (8 oz, 250 g) of sugar. Bring to the boil again, adding the water in which the seeds were soaked – the pectin from the seeds will be present in the water and will help the marmalade to set. Boil the mixture rapidly, stirring all the time, until it forms tiny bubbles and jells when tested. Store in sterilized jars. This quantity should fill two 1-lb (500-g) jars.

## TANGERINE MARMALADE

This is an extremely delicate, exquisite marmalade.

2 lb (1 kg) tangerines                         4¼ cups (2¼ lb, 1.1 kg) sugar

Wash the fruit carefully and cut them in half. Squeeze the juice into a bowl and refrigerate. Remove the inner skin from the rind and discard. Put all the rind in a large pan of water and simmer for 15 minutes or until it is quite tender, then drain and discard the water. Place the rind in fresh water and leave it to soak for at least 10 hours, changing the water 2 or 3 times to get rid of the bitterness.

Drain the rind and cut it into very thin slices. Put it in a heavy saucepan with the tangerine juice and the sugar. Bring to the boil, then lower the heat and simmer until the syrup thickens and jells when tested in cold water. It will take about 30–45 minutes. While still warm, but not too hot, transfer the marmalade to warm sterilized jars. This quantity should fill three 1-lb (500-g) jars.

## BANANA JAM

Here is a good way of using up surplus ripe bananas.

3 cups (1½ lb, 750 g) sugar          juice of 3 limes
1 cup (8 fl oz, 250 ml) water        6 ripe bananas

Place the sugar, water and lime juice in a saucepan and bring to the boil, then reduce the heat and add the chopped bananas. Simmer for approximately 30–45 minutes, or until the jam thickens. Transfer to warm sterilized jars. This quantity should fill two 1-lb (500-g) jars.

## MANGO JAM

slightly under-ripe mangoes      sugar
water

Peel the mangoes and cut the flesh from the seeds. Put the mango pieces to boil in just sufficient water to cover them, and cook for 30 minutes or until they are tender. Remove from the heat, pour the contents of the pan into a sieve over a bowl, and rub the mango slices vigorously until only the stringy bits remain in the sieve. Measure the mixture in the bowl, and to every cup (8 fl oz, 250 ml) add 1 cup (8 oz, 250 g) of sugar. Bring to the boil again, then reduce the heat and simmer until the jam jells. While still warm, transfer it to warm sterilized jars.

## PINEAPPLE JAM

2 cups grated fresh pineapple (1 pineapple approx. 2½–3 lb, 1.25 kg)

1 cup (8 fl oz, 250 ml) water
1½ cups (12 oz, 350 g) sugar
juice of 1 lime

Cook the pineapple gently in the water until it is tender. Add the sugar and lime juice, and simmer until the mixture thickens and sets when tested in a little cold water. Transfer to warm sterilized jars. This quantity should fill two 1-lb (500-g) jars.

## SORREL JAM

2 lb (1 kg) sorrel petals          6 cups (3 lb, 1.5 kg) sugar
4 cups (1½ pints, 1 litre) water

Wash the sorrel well to get rid of any dirt and grit, and boil it in the water until it is quite tender. Add the sugar, mix well, and simmer until the mixture jells when tested in cold water. Transfer to warm sterilized jars. This quantity should fill four 1-lb (500-g) jars.

## GARDEN CHERRY JAM

These little red berries, high in Vitamin C, are also known as acerola, Barbados cherries or West Indian cherries. They make excellent jams and jellies.

4 cups (2 lb, 1 kg) garden cherries     sugar
4 cups (1½ pints, 1 litre) water

Place the garden cherries and water in a saucepan. Bring to the boil, then lower the heat and simmer for 10 minutes. Remove the pan from the heat and press the fruit through a sieve. For every cup (8 fl oz, 250 ml) of the resulting purée or pulp, add 1 cup (8 oz, 250 g) of sugar. Return it to the heat, bring to the boil, and gently simmer the mixture until it thickens. Transfer to warm sterilized jars. This quantity makes about 2½ lb (1.25 kg) of jam.

## GARDEN CHERRY JELLY

4 cups (2 lb, 1 kg) garden cherries     sugar
4 cups (1½ pints, 1 litre) water

Lightly crush the garden cherries and place them in a saucepan with the water. Bring to the boil, then reduce the heat and simmer for 30 minutes. Strain the juice through a muslin cloth, taking care not to press the cherries. For every cup (8 fl oz, 250 ml) of the resulting liquid, add a cup (8 oz, 250 g) of sugar. Return the pan to the heat and boil rapidly until the mixture jells. Transfer to warm sterilized jars. This quantity should make 2 lb (1 kg) jelly.

## HOG PLUM JELLY

These thin-fleshed, large-seeded yellow plums are not often seen for sale. The large trees are to be found growing along country roads. When in season, the plums lie scattered under the trees, perfuming the air with their pungent sweet smell.

| | |
|---|---|
| hog plums | sugar |
| water | |

Wash the plums well and place them in a saucepan with sufficient water to cover. Bring to the boil, then lower the heat and simmer for 30 minutes. Strain the fruit and juice, making sure that you do not crush the plums. Discard the fruit. Measure the liquid, and for every cup (8 fl oz, 250 ml) of it add 1 cup (8 oz, 250 g) of sugar. Bring to the boil again and continue to boil rapidly until the mixture reaches setting point. Transfer to warm sterilized jars.

## GUAVA JELLY

| | |
|---|---|
| guavas | sugar |
| water | lime juice |

Choose firm but ripe guavas. Wash them and cut them in half, then put them to boil in a large pan with just enough water to cover. Boil them gently for 30 minutes until they are tender.

Pour the contents of the pan into a large sieve lined with muslin, placed over a bowl. You may have to do several batches, depending on how much fruit is being cooked. (The traditional way of straining the guavas is to tie a muslin cloth to the legs of an upturned chair. The contents of the pot are poured into the muslin and the juice drips through and is caught by a bowl placed underneath it.)

Measure the juice, and for every cup (8 fl oz, 250 ml) of it add 1 cup (8 oz, 250 g) of sugar. Add the juice of 1 lime for every 3 cups (1¼ pints, 750 ml) of the liquid. Return the mixture to the pan and boil vigorously, stirring occasionally, until small bubbles begin to appear and the jelly forms little balls when tested in cold water. Let it cool slightly, then pour it into warm sterilized jars.

## MANGO JELLY

mangoes | cloves (optional)
water | sugar

Choose mature but under-ripe mangoes. Peel and slice them, discarding the seeds, and put them in a pan with just sufficient water to cover them. Add a few cloves if you like, and boil for about 30 minutes, until the mangoes are tender.

Strain through a sieve lined with muslin cloth, but do not press the fruit as this will make the jelly cloudy. To every cup (8 fl oz, 250 ml) of the liquid add 1 cup (8 oz, 250 g) of sugar. Return the mixture to the pan and boil it rapidly until it sets. Pour into warm sterilized jars.

## SORREL JELLY

whole sorrel fruit – petals and | water
  seeds | sugar

Wash the fruit well, and place it in a large saucepan with just enough water to cover. Boil for 1 hour or until the fruit is soft.

Strain the juice and fruit through a muslin-lined sieve, and to every cup (8 fl oz, 250 ml) of the strained liquid add 1 cup (8 oz, 250 g) of sugar. Boil the liquid and sugar rapidly until the mixture jells when tested in cold water. Pour into warm sterilized jars.

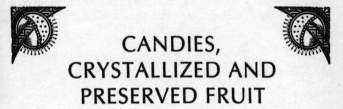

# CANDIES,
# CRYSTALLIZED AND
# PRESERVED FRUIT

# ✸CANDIES

Not many years ago, both in the city and in country areas, candy vendors were to be seen everywhere with their show cases full of striped red and white peppermints, sugar or grater cakes and other sweets. A favourite spot was the piazza at the top of King Street at South Parade in Kingston. But in recent years these vendors have all disappeared and, unfortunately, peppermint candy seems almost to have become a thing of the past.

I have tried to include recipes for all the old favourites in this section, as well as others which might not be well known.

## PEPPERMINT CANDY

The decline in the art of making these candies is perhaps due on the one hand to the availability of mass-produced sweets, and on the other to the secrecy and mystique surrounding the making of them. I was told that one had to pay to be initiated into the art, and, once learned, it was a closely kept secret.

The candy was made entirely by sight and feel. Success depended on timing and dexterity in manipulating the hot flowing mass. Perhaps this is why there was such a mystique and ritual attached to its production. For example, no new person was allowed into the area of the candy-making once the operation had started. If anyone in the group had to leave suddenly for some reason, but wished to return later, this person must look into the saucepan before departing. Some lime juice must be sprinkled around the table on which the candy would be worked, to get rid of smells. This, I think, was also intended to ward off spirits or the evil eye.

The following recipe, slightly adjusted, was demonstrated for me by Thelma Rowe of Kingston, who learned the art at an early age.

| Ingredients | Equipment |
|---|---|
| 4 cups (2 lb, 1 kg) granulated cane sugar | oiled 6-in (15-cm) nail driven into a post |
| 1¼ cups (½ pint, 300 ml) water | medium-sized, wide, heavy saucepan |
| ½ teaspoon lime *or* lemon juice | candy thermometer |
| ¼ teaspoon red food colouring | pastry brush |
| 1 teaspoon essence of peppermint oil | marble or stone slab or table, wetted |
| | baking sheet, lightly oiled |
| | pair of scissors, blades oiled |

Combine the sugar, water and lime or lemon juice in the saucepan. Clip on the thermometer. Bring the mixture to the boil over a moderately high heat, stirring it until all the sugar is dissolved. Stop stirring as soon as it begins to boil. From time to time, using a pastry brush dipped in water, remove any impurities or crystals that may form on the sides of the saucepan. Boil the mixture for 30 minutes or until it reaches the soft crack stage, 280°F, 138°C. (If a spoonful of the mixture poured into very cold water hardens and can be snapped, then it has reached the soft crack stage.) Remove the pan immediately from the heat.

Pour most of the mixture – leaving about 1 cup in the saucepan – on to the marble or stone slab or table, which should have been scrubbed clean and dampened with water to prevent sticking. Put the saucepan with the rest of the mixture back on a very low heat. Add the red food colouring, stir well, and leave on the heat.

In a few minutes the edges of the mixture poured on to the slab will start to harden; lift it with a knife, all round the edge, rolling inwards little by little as the mixture cools, until you have a ball of fairly hot clear sugar.

Oil your hands and quickly place the ball of sugar over the oiled nail. Work the sugar by pulling it downwards as far as it will go, then hooking the end over the nail again. Repeat the process until the sugar becomes completely white – about 5–10 minutes. Add the essence of peppermint from the top and repeat the pulling–throwing process twice more, so that the peppermint is well distributed over the mass. (Alternatively you could just keep pulling and stretching the candy by hand, without using a nail, until it turns white, and then add the peppermint and manipulate again to distribute it.)

Quickly place the candy on the baking sheet and keep it warm in a very low oven. This is to prevent it from hardening too quickly.

Now pour the hot red mixture that was left in the saucepan on to the dampened marble top. As it cools, pull up the edges as before and roll it into a little ball. Cover it with a small bowl to keep it warm.

Cut off one-third of the white candy in the oven, using scissors with oiled blades, and pull it into a long even cylinder shape about 2 inches (5 cm) in diameter. Put a little oil on the marble table to prevent the candy from sticking, lay the white candy on it, then quickly take up one-third of the red candy and work it by pulling and stretching it to form a piece the same length as the white candy, but much thinner. Place the red firmly on the white candy so that they stick together.

Starting from the end, make four cuts, 1 inch (2.5 cm) apart, to three-quarters of the depth of the candy, so that each segment is still attached to the next. Cut completely through at the fifth cut, and quickly make a ring by joining the ends. Repeat the process until all the candy is used up.

Long candy sticks are traditionally made by clipping the strips of red and white candy into desired lengths and twisting them. You can choose which you prefer, or try both.

The whole process is fast and calls for a certain amount of dexterity. After a couple of attempts, you should get the feel of it.


## PEANUT BRITTLE

Wangla nuts (sesame seeds) were at one time also used to make brittle. These 'wanglas' were very popular but are now rarely seen.

2 cups (1 lb, 500 g) sugar
½ cup (4 oz, 125 ml) water
½ teaspoon cream of tartar
¼ teaspoon bicarbonate of soda

¼ teaspoon salt
2 tablespoons (1 oz, 30 g) butter
1 cup (6 oz, 175 g) peanuts

Combine the sugar, water and cream of tartar in a heavy sauce-pan. Boil the mixture until it reaches the crack stage, 310°F, 155°C. Remove it from the heat and quickly add the soda, salt, butter and peanuts. Pour the mixture into a greased flat container and cut it into pieces while it is still warm.

## GINGER CANDIES

2 cups (1 lb, 500 g) sugar
¼ cup (2 fl oz, 50 ml) water
3 tablespoons grated fresh ginger

1 teaspoon lime juice
1 teaspoon butter

Combine the sugar, water and ginger in a thick saucepan and boil the mixture until it forms a firm ball when tested in cold water. (If you use a thermometer, boil to crack stage, 295°F, 145°C.) Quickly remove it from the heat and add the lime juice and butter, beating them in well. Pour the mixture into a greased flat container and cut into pieces while it is still warm.

## PAWPAW BALLS

2 cups (10 oz, 300 g) unripe
  pawpaw, grated
2½ cups (1¼ lb, 600 g) sugar
¼ cup (2 fl oz, 50 ml) water

1 tablespoon lime juice
½ teaspoon grated lime rind
colouring (optional)

Boil the grated pawpaw in a saucepan of water for 3 minutes, then strain and discard the water. Repeat this process again. Press out as much of the liquid as you can from the cooked pawpaw, discard the juice and set aside the pawpaw flesh.

In the meantime, make a syrup by simmering the sugar and ¼ cup of water until the mixture forms a thread when tested in cold water (240°F, 118°C). Add the pawpaw flesh to the syrup and continue to simmer until the mixture leaves the side of the saucepan. Stir in the lime juice and the grated lime peel and leave to cool. Shape it into balls, colour them if you like, and roll them in some sugar. Store in sterilized jars.

## TAMARIND BALLS

tamarinds                                     sugar

Shell the tamarinds and scrape out the pulp. To every cup (½ lb, 250 g) of pulp, add 2 cups (1 lb, 500 g) of sugar, or add enough sugar to the pulp to make it hold together without being sticky. Mix well. Shape into little balls, roll them in sugar, and store them in sterilized jars.

## GUAVA CHEESE

guavas                                        sugar
water

Chop the guavas coarsely, and steam them in a little water until they are tender. Drain them well, press them through a sieve, and to each cup (8 fl oz, 250 ml) of the resulting pulp add 1 cup (8 oz, 250 g) of sugar. Place the pulp and the sugar in a wide, heavy, shallow saucepan, and boil over a medium heat, stirring constantly until the mixture thickens and leaves the sides of the saucepan.

Pour the mixture into a damp shallow container and when it is nearly cold and has set, cut into squares. If it has not set when cold, then pour it all back into the saucepan and continue to cook until it thickens some more. Coat each piece with sifted icing sugar. They will keep for a long time if stored in sterilized jars.

## MANGO CHEESE

firm ripe mangoes (no. 11s)                   sugar

Use no. 11 mangoes as they are not too hairy and have a good flavour. The name comes from the fact that this variety carried the number 11 tag in the collection taken from a French ship by H.M.S. *Flora* in 1782 (see p. 137).

Peel the mangoes and cut the flesh from the seeds. Rub the flesh through a sieve or purée in a blender. Measure the pulp or purée, and to every cup (8 fl oz, 250 ml) of it add 1 cup (8 oz, 250 g) of sugar. Cook the pulp and sugar in a heavy, wide, shallow saucepan until the mixture thickens and shrinks from the sides of the pan.

Pour the mixture into a shallow damp container while it is still hot. When nearly cold, cut into squares, and later, when they are quite cold, dip them in sifted icing sugar. Store them in airtight tins or sterilized jars. They will keep for a long time.

## COCONUT SUGAR CAKE

3 cups (1½ lb, 750 g) granulated sugar  
½ cup (4 fl oz, 125 ml) water

2 cups (8 oz, 250 g) grated coconut, dark skin removed  
red or green colouring

Combine the sugar and water in a heavy shallow saucepan. Bring the mixture to the boil over a medium heat and stir until a light syrup has formed. Add the grated coconut, and keep stirring until the mixture holds together but is still moist. Immediately remove the pan from the heat and drop spoonfuls of the mixture on to a greased dish. Leave a little of it in the pan, and if it has become too sugary or set add a little water to it. Return the pan to the heat for a minute, stir, then add a drop or two of red or green food colouring. Stir again, then put a little of this mixture on each of the already spooned out cakes.

They will look extremely pretty, red and white or green and white. If you find that the cakes have not set, then scrape everything back into the saucepan and recook. Because of the addition of the food colouring the second attempt will produce all pink or all green cakes! When you have made them once or twice you will get the feel of it.

## ORANGE SWEETMEATS

Here is a delightful recipe, dating from 1809, according to Caroline Sullivan's *Jamaica Cookery Book* (1893).

'Whole seville oranges, equal weight of granulated sugar

Boil the seville oranges, whole, in two or three different sets of water until the bitterness is gone. Cut them and take out the pulp and juice; then beat the outside very fine in a mortar and put to it an equal weight of granulated sugar. When extremely well mixed to a paste, spread it thin on china dishes and set them in the sun or before the fire. When half dry, cut it into what form you please, turn the other side up and dry that. Keep them in a box with layers of paper. They are for dessert; and are also useful as a stomachic, to carry in the pockets for journeys, or for gentlemen when shooting, or for gouty subjects.'

# ✳PRESERVED FRUIT

## BANANA FIGS

These make excellent additions to puddings and cakes and are also delicious as dried fruit.

Choose big ripe bananas, peel them, and put them to dry in the sun on a wire rack. Cover them with a thin piece of muslin to keep off the flies. Turn them once a day, continuing the process for at least a week or until they are quite dry and brown. At the end of each day take them indoors to prevent the dew gathering on them. Pack them in airtight tins with some waxed paper between the layers. They will keep indefinitely.

## BREADFRUIT BLOSSOM PRESERVES

The blossoms of the breadfruit tree, or swords, as they are called, fall to the ground and are usually left to rot. But they can be made into a delicious preserve.

12 breadfruit blossoms  
2 cups (1 lb, 500 g) sugar  

1 cup (8 fl oz, 250 ml) water

Gather the blossoms while they are still fresh and plump, soak them in some water for 15 minutes, then scrape off the rough outer skin. Put them in a saucepan with enough water to cover them. Bring to the boil and cook them until they are tender, then discard the water. In the meantime prepare a thick syrup with the sugar and water. Add the blossoms to the syrup and continue to cook them gently until they have absorbed most of it. Dry them in the sun as described in the previous recipe.

## PRESERVED TAMARINDS

6 cups (2¼ lb, 1.1 kg) brown
  sugar
2½ cups (1 pint, 600 ml) water

2 lb (1 kg) tamarinds, shells
  removed

Make a heavy syrup with the sugar and water, and add the shelled tamarinds, turning them over in the syrup so that they are completely coated with it. Remove the pot from the heat. While still warm, pour the tamarinds into sterilized warmed jars. They will keep indefinitely.

## ✳ CANDIED AND CRYSTALLIZED FRUIT

To drink between meals may not be forbidden in a hot country as this, for whoso lists may properly take a plentiful draught of water, as it is usual for some before they take their chocolata, but by no means soon after, as strictly prohibited by the observing Spaniard. However at other times a large draught of the pure crystalline naturally well concocted water, may well refresh and contribute to render our bloods thin, and circulate the better; and lest such at sometimes should chill the stomach too much, the Spanish custome of eating candid warm Fruits and Roots after such draughts may be esteemed reasonable, such as candied limes, oranges, ginger, marmalade of Guvas, quiddimes of Citrons to be taken in little quantities as we usually do cheese after meat for concoction.

Thomas Trapham,
*A discourse on the State of Health
in the Island of Jamaica*, 1679

Candied and crystallized fruits are relatively simple to make, although the preparation may span a period of several days. The end product is worth the time spent, as the fruit and peel make attractive decorations for desserts. They can also be served on their own. They make splendid gifts when packed in attractive containers.

METHOD

The process of candying fruit consists of soaking it in a hot sweet syrup, the sweetness of which is increased daily until the fruit is totally impregnated with the syrup. Crystallization is one step further in the process – the candied fruit is dipped in boiling water, drained and rolled in sugar.

SUITABLE FRUITS

Only firm fresh fruits are suitable for this lengthy process, for example pineapples, otaheite apples, cashews, grapes and certain citrus peels. Roots such as ginger also make ideal items for crystallization.

# CANDIED FRUIT

Peel the fruit and cut it into small pieces. It is advisable to process each kind of fruit separately, as the individual flavour may otherwise be lost. Weigh the fruit, place it in a large saucepan, and cover it with water. Bring to the boil, then simmer until the fruit is tender but still firm. Drain the pieces of fruit, reserving the liquid, and place them in a large heat-proof, non-metallic bowl.

*Syrup*

For every 1 lb (500 g) of fruit, make a syrup from 1¼ cups (½ pint, 300 ml) of the reserved liquid, plus ¾ cup (6 oz, 175 g) of sugar *or* ¼ cup (2 oz, 50 g) of sugar and ½ cup (4 oz, 125 ml) of liquid glucose. (Glucose gives better results than sugar. You can also use 2 tablespoons of lime or lemon juice to replace the glucose.) Bring the sugar and liquid to the boil and cook until a thin syrup forms.

*Candying Process*

Pour the hot syrup over the fruit, making sure that it is well covered by the syrup.

The next day pour off the syrup and add to it a further ¼ cup (2 oz, 50 g) of sugar. Bring it to the boil and pour it over the fruit again. Repeat this process for 2 more days, remembering to add the extra sugar each time.

On the fifth day, drain the syrup into a saucepan and add ⅜ cup (3 oz, 75 g) of sugar. Add the fruit and boil for 3 minutes; return the fruit and syrup to the heatproof container and leave for a further 2 days.

Repeat the last process once again. Leave the fruit in the syrup for 4 days.

Now remove the fruit with a slotted spoon. Place it on a rack with a container beneath to catch the excess syrup. Dry the fruit either in the sun, with a piece of muslin cloth thrown over to keep away the flies, or in a very slow oven.

# ✳ TO CRYSTALLIZE CANDIED FRUIT

Dip the dry candied fruit into some boiling water, drain very well, then roll each piece in granulated sugar.

# CANDIED PEEL

Choose bright-coloured citrus fruit, such as tangerines, grape-fruit and limes. Remove the peel and weigh it. Place the peel in a large saucepan and cover with cold water. Bring to the boil, then reduce the heat and simmer until tender. Drain the peel, reserving the liquid. Place the peel in a heatproof container.

For each 1 lb (500 g) of peel, make a syrup from 1¼ cups (½ pint, 300 ml) of the reserved liquid, plus 1 cup (8 oz, 250 g) of sugar, *or* ½ cup (4 oz, 125 g) of sugar and ½ cup (4 oz, 125 g) of glucose. Bring to the boil and cook until it makes a thin syrup. Pour it over the peel and leave for 24 hours.

Next, pour the syrup into a saucepan and add ½ cup (4 oz, 125 g) of sugar. Bring to the boil, cook for 1 minute, then pour the syrup over the peel. The next day put the syrup and the peel in a saucepan, bring it to the boil and simmer gently until the peel is transparent – about 30 minutes. Remove the peel with a slotted spoon and dry on a rack with a container beneath to catch the dripping syrup. Dry either in the sun, covered with a piece of muslin cloth, or in the oven set at the lowest temperature.

Store in sterilized jars. The candies will keep for many months.

## CANDIED GINGER

The best ginger, tender and plump, is harvested during the months of December and January. Use only the plumpest and freshest roots.

Weigh the ginger roots, and put them to boil in a large pot of water until they are tender. Cool them in cold water and then scrape off the outer skin. Place the ginger in a bowl and cover with plenty of fresh cold water. Leave for 2 days, changing the water two or three times. This removes the heat from the ginger.

For every 1 lb (500 g) of ginger, make a thin syrup from ¾ cup (6 oz, 175 g) of sugar and 1¼ cups (½ pint, 300 ml) of water. Drain the ginger and place it in a non-metallic heatproof container. Pour the hot syrup over the ginger, and leave it for a day. Next, make a second, thicker batch of syrup from 1 heaped cup (9 oz, 250 g) of sugar and 1¼ cups (½ pint, 300 ml) of water. Set aside the previous syrup or keep it to make into a drink. Pour the new hot syrup over the ginger and leave for a day, then drain off and set aside this syrup.

Finally, make a very thick syrup from 2 cups (1 lb, 500 g) of sugar and 1¼ cups (½ pint, 300 ml) of water. This time leave the syrup until it is *cold* before pouring it over the drained ginger, and leave for a day.

Remove the ginger from the syrup and dry it as described in the previous recipes. The syrups used during the process can be bottled and diluted with water to make a pleasant cooling ginger drink.

# PICKLES

A jar of hot pickles is always available in most Jamaican homes, to sprinkle over meats, fish and salads. Relatives living or studying abroad send urgent messages home for these hot pickles to be dispatched to them.

## PICKLED PEPPERS

12 hot red peppers
12 hot green peppers
12 hot yellow peppers

2½ cups (1 pint, 600 ml) vinegar
1 teaspoon salt
2 tablespoons pimento berries

Cut the peppers into slices and place them in sterilized jars. Bring the vinegar to the boil, and add the salt and the pimento berries. Allow to cool, then pour over the peppers in the jar. Screw on the tops tightly and store them until they are needed.

## CALABASH PICKLED

The calabash (*Crescentia cujete*) is a hard gourd, often used as a container for food or water. Until I came across this recipe in Caroline Sullivan's *Jamaica Cookery Book* (1893) I had no idea that it was edible.

1 very young, small calabash
salt
vinegar

pimento berries
hot peppers

Cut the calabash into four pieces, sprinkle them with salt, and leave until the fruit turns black. Wash it to get rid of the excess salt. Boil together some vinegar, pimento berries and sliced hot peppers. Pour this over the calabash when cool, and store in sterilized jars.

# MANGO CHUTNEY

| | |
|---|---|
| 12 mature mangoes | 1⅓ cups (8 oz, 250 g) raisins |
| 2 oz (50 g) green ginger | ¼ cup (2 oz, 50 g) salt |
| 1 clove garlic | 1 cup (8 oz, 250 g) sugar |
| 4 oz (125 g) shelled tamarinds | 2 cups (¾ pint, 500 ml) vinegar |
| 1 hot pepper | |

Wash and peel the mangoes. Cut them into small pieces and discard the seeds. Mince the ginger and garlic or chop them very finely. Scrape the pulp from the tamarinds, and chop the hot pepper finely, discarding the seeds.

Place the ginger, garlic, tamarind pulp, hot pepper and mango pieces in a saucepan with the raisins, salt, sugar and vinegar. Bring to the boil, then lower the heat and simmer until the mixture thickens. Stir it from time to time to prevent it sticking and burning. Pour into warm sterilized jars.

# CURING AND
PICKLING MEAT AND
SALTING FISH

# * CURING AND PICKLING MEAT

Our economy was, from the sixteenth to the nineteenth century, a plantation economy. This meant that plantations were allied to British merchant houses, which supplied them with capital and goods in exchange for the sale of sugar on the British market. Even as the economy changed, we still depended on the traditional sources for goods which we did not produce ourselves, but had become accustomed to enjoying. All our hams, sausages, bacon, salted meats and fish continued to be imported, although we were producing, for example, excellent pork.

In the 1970s, owing to the severe decline in the economy, we attempted for the first time to become self-sufficient. Processing of pork products began to expand, and the curing of hams and bacon was discovered by many to be after all a very simple process.

Meat is cured by the addition of three main ingredients: salt, spices and saltpetre. Salt is the most important curing agent, spices add flavour, and saltpetre gives the meat an appetizing red colour without which it would look dull and grey. After the meat has been impregnated with these ingredients it is left for some time for the cure to take place. It is often smoked after the curing process.

There are two main methods of curing meat: the dry cure and the brine cure. For the dry cure the meat is rubbed with the curing mixture and turned over often, sometimes once a day, until the curing is complete. For the brine cure, a brine solution is made by adding cooled boiled water to the curing mixture. The meat is lowered into it so as to be completely submerged if unrefrigerated and covered with a lid. The half-and-half method is also used. Some spiced brine solution is pumped into the meat, especially around the bone areas, and the outside of the meat is rubbed with the dry curing mixture.

From earliest times, the inhabitants of our island have preserved meat. The buccaneers learned from the Indians how to barbecue or smoke meat, and they in turn used this method to preserve large quantities of wild meat to sell to passing ships. A simpler method of smoking was practised by later inhabitants of

Jamaica. The kitchen, which was usually separate from the house, used wood for fuel. Over the wood fire, fairly high up, was hung a wire basket called a 'kreng kreng', filled with various pieces of meat. The meat was left there to be smoked over a period and was used to flavour and enrich stews and soups.

Once cured or smoked, meat should be kept in the refrigerator and used within 2 weeks, or frozen for later use.

## CORNED BEEF

Our corned beef is very similar to the spiced beef which was popular in seventeenth-century English cooking. It was then a regular Christmas dish, to be found on the tables of many English country houses and farms. Various forms of it have been known for at least 300 years, in such areas as Yorkshire, Cumberland, Wales and Sussex.

Our corned beef is different from the salted English silverside or salt beef, as ours is highly spiced.

| | |
|---|---|
| 12 pimento berries | 1 teaspoon thyme leaves |
| 2 stalks escallion, chopped | 3 tablespoons salt |
| 3 slices hot pepper | ½ teaspoon saltpetre |
| 1 clove garlic | 3 lb (1.5 kg) leg, loin or silverside |
| 1 teaspoon black pepper | of beef |

Pound the pimento berries in a mortar. Add the escallion, hot pepper and garlic and pound these almost to a purée, then combine with the black pepper, thyme, salt and saltpetre and mix well.

With a sharp, long, narrow-bladed knife, make incisions all over the meat. Place a little of the seasoning mixture in each incision, leaving some to rub over the outside of the meat.

Place the seasoned meat in a glass, china or earthenware container, cover with plastic wrap, and leave it for 2–3 days in the bottom of the refrigerator. Turn it over once or twice during this period.

When the meat is to be cooked, transfer it to a large pot with plenty of water. Bring it to the boil, then lower the heat and gently cook it until it is tender. This should take about 2 hours. The corned beef should be tender but not falling apart. Serve it hot, with potato salad, mustard and pickles. Enough for 4.

## CORNED OX TONGUE

1 tongue, 2–3 lb (1–1.5 kg)
1 tablespoon pimento berries
½ hot pepper, chopped
1 stalk escallion, chopped

½ teaspoon thyme leaves
3 tablespoons salt
½ teaspoon saltpetre

Wash the tongue and dry it. Pound the pimento berries in a mortar, then add the chopped hot pepper, escallion and thyme leaves and continue to pound. Add the salt and saltpetre, and mix well. Rub this mixture over the tongue, then place it in a non-metallic container and leave it in the bottom of the refrigerator for 2–3 days, turning it once or twice.

Boil the tongue in a large pan of water for about 2 hours, until it is tender. When it is to be served, take it out of the pot, place it on a carving board, and strip off the coarse outer skin, which should come off easily. Cut it into slices and serve hot. Like corned beef, it goes very well with potato salad, pickles, mustard and the following sauce.

Chop a large onion and a clove of garlic, and sauté them in a little oil for a minute or two on a medium heat. Add a large chopped tomato and stir. Throw in 3 tablespoons of vinegar, salt and pepper to taste, and 2 tablespoons of water. Simmer for 5 minutes. The sauce should be prepared in advance so that no time is wasted in getting the hot tongue to the table.

## CORNED PORK

Use the same method and proportions as given in the recipe for corned ox tongue, above.

## PICKLED MEAT

To pickle meat such as pig's tail and beef, all that is required is a strong brine made with salt, saltpetre and spices.

*for 5–6 lb (2.5–3 kg) of meat:*
2 lb (1 kg) salt
¾ oz (20 g) saltpetre

15 cups (6 pints, 3.5 litres) water
3 tablespoons pimento berries

Place all the ingredients in a pan, stir well, and bring to the boil. Simmer for 10 minutes, then leave until quite cool. Place the meat in a non-metallic container, preferably glass or earthenware, pour the brine over it, and refrigerate. The curing time will be 1½ days per pound (500 g) of meat. Turn the meat over once a day so that the solution will penetrate it evenly.

## CURING A HAM

This is one of the very many recipes that exist for the curing of ham. Some recipes use beer, molasses and various spices.

METHOD 1
¾ oz (20 g) saltpetre
5 cups (2 pints, 1.25 litres) beer
1 cup molasses
3 tablespoons pimento berries,
  crushed

1 small piece of ginger
10–12 lb (5–6 kg) pork leg

Put the first five ingredients in a saucepan, bring to the boil, remove from the heat and allow to cool. Wipe the leg of pork clean with a cloth dipped in vinegar, pour over the cool liquid, and refrigerate. The curing time will be 2 days per 1 lb (500 g) of meat. Turn the meat every other day so that each side is well saturated with the brine.

If the ham is to be smoked, remove it from the brine, wipe it dry and weigh it. To smoke, hang it near a hardwood fire or in a smoke box, which should not generate heat higher than 75–85°F, 24–29°C. Twenty-four hours of continuous smoking should produce a 25 per cent weight loss, which indicates that smoking is complete.

METHOD 2

In most supermarkets one will find a prepared curing mixture called 'Morton's Tender Quick'. This is how I use it.

*Infusion*

1 cup (8 fl oz, 250 ml) boiling water

2 cinnamon sticks

20 pimento berries

1 small piece of fresh ginger, crushed

a few coriander seeds (optional)

Pour the boiling water over the spices and leave to infuse for at least 1 hour or until cool. Strain and set aside.

### Preparing the pork leg

Wipe the pork carefully with a clean cloth steeped in vinegar. If it is frozen, allow it to thaw completely. You will need 1 oz (25 g) of 'Morton's Tender Quick' per 1 lb (500 g) of meat. Add a quarter of the total amount of Morton's Tender Quick to the cooled spice infusion. Inject this solution all over the pork, especially around the bone area where bacteria are likely to develop. A meat pump is generally used to inject the solution into the meat, but a plastic oil baster with a long narrow spout can be used successfully. If the latter is to be used, make incisions all over the pork, especially around the bone areas, and squirt the infusion into the incisions, repeating where necessary.

Add ½ cup (3 oz, 75 g) of brown sugar to the remaining 'Tender Quick' mixture, and rub it all over the outside of the pork, making quite sure that the whole leg has been coated.

Wrap the pork in waxed paper and tie it securely, then wrap it in several layers of newspaper. Put it in a large plastic bag and tie the top. Place it on the bottom shelf of the refrigerator, in a long container to catch any of the solution that might drip out of the bag. Turn it over every other day. An average sized leg of pork takes approximately 4 weeks to be cured. Curing time is usually 2 days per 1 lb (500 g) of meat.

If the ham is to be eaten plainly boiled, it will take about 3 hours depending on the size (allow about 15 minutes per 1 lb/500 g). If it is to be baked, first boil it for 1 hour to get rid of some of the salt, then transfer it to the oven and bake until it is tender, about 2 hours.

## TO MAKE BACON

Ask your butcher for the bacon cut or loin of pork. Use the brine solution given for the ham in the recipe above, or the following 'Morton's Tender Quick' method.

For every 1 lb (500 g) of meat use 1 oz (25 g) of 'Tender Quick'. Add a little sugar and some coarsely pounded pimento berries to it, and rub this mixture thoroughly into the bacon cut. Wrap it in waxed paper and newspaper as described in the previous recipe, then place it in a plastic bag and tie the top. Refrigerate, turning it over every day. Curing time is 1½ days per 1 lb (500 g) of meat.

Smoke in the same way as ham (see p. 220) if desired.

## SAUSAGES

Clean the pig's intestines carefully by washing them several times, turning them inside out with a long stick and scraping the slime away. Leave them to soak overnight or for 12 hours in a mild solution of salt and water with the juice of 2 limes added.

When you are ready to use the intestines, wash them and dry with a clean kitchen cloth or paper.

To every 2 lb (1 kg) of minced pork, add 3 tablespoons of salt, 2 teaspoons of freshly ground black pepper, 1–2 hot peppers chopped fine, without their seeds, 1 chopped clove of garlic and ¼ teaspoon of saltpetre. Mix the minced pork and spices very well, and stuff the intestines with the mixture, tying the sausages with some string at intervals. Place them in a plastic bag and leave at the bottom of the refrigerator for 3–4 days, after which they should be ready to be grilled, barbecued or simply boiled.

If the sausages are to be barbecued, add some green aromatic wood such as mango or pimento to the fire to give them a delicious flavour. These sausages are so much tastier than those we can buy here that they are well worth the effort.

# ❋ SALTING FISH

The salting of fish is also a very simple process. The fish is washed, salted and put to dry in the sun, covered with a piece of muslin cloth to keep away the flies. Smoked fish is made in the same way as smoked meat.

I feel very guilty about giving recipes for salt fish, first because all fish is best eaten when fresh and secondly because fresh fish is more expensive. However, in recent times imported salt fish has been hard to come by, and as many of our best dishes call for it, the cook may have to produce a substitute.

| | |
|---|---|
| 2 lb (1 kg) fish | 2 cups (1 lb, 500 g) salt |

Have the heads and entrails of the fish removed. Make 3 gashes across each fish, and rub the salt all over them, working it in well. Leave the fish in a large non-metallic container for a day. By then a brine will have formed, which should be thrown away. Wipe the fish dry and put them in the sun on a raised mat which will allow some air to flow under them. Keep turning them until they are dry. The process may take several days, and they must be brought in at night. A muslin cloth thrown over them will keep off the flies. Watch out for cats!

# MEDICINALS
# AND HERB TEAS

This is not an attempt to delve into the wide area of folk medicine, but only to give a few recipes for the general and safe use of a few common herbs.

The dominant part of our folk medicine is of West African origin. During the slave period, Myal men or native doctors were versed in the art of bush medicine and its preparation, learnt in Africa. Many slaves would allow themselves to be treated only by these doctors. Monk Lewis's slave, Bessie, for example, told him flatly that 'the white doctor could do her no good'. Later, Lewis writes: 'I find that Bessie's black doctor is really nothing more than a professor of medicine as to this particular disease; and I have ordered her to be sent to him in the mountains immediately' (*Journal of a West Indian Proprietor*, 1834).

Folk medicine is built up around tradition and superstition. It is still practised by a wide cross-section of the population, and transcends class and race structures in Jamaica.

Some of the plants used as bush teas have been the subject of research, and some of them have proven medicinal properties. Some, on the other hand, have been found to be harmful.

It was common practice during my childhood for children to be given various tonics. I vividly recall one which was made from rice bitters (*Andrographis paniculata*) and other herbs. This bitter brew was given just before we were sent to bed, and I can remember pretending to be asleep from early evening so as to be spared from having to take this dreadful-tasting brew. It was also common practice to give a 'wash out' in the form of a dose of castor oil before children returned to school after the summer holidays. This, it was felt, was needed to purge the system of all the mangoes and rubbish that were eaten during the summer.

It is said that my maternal grandfather never ate a meal outside his house before taking a dose of bissy and rum, a supposed antidote for poison. This he carried everywhere with him.

Here are some of the normal household uses of a few of these herbs and other plants:

## PAWPAW LEAVES (Carica papaya)

Meats are wrapped in the pawpaw leaves to be tenderized.

## FEVER (LEMON) GRASS TEA

This is a very fragrant, lemony-smelling grass which is used extensively in the cooking of South East Asia. In Jamaica it is used only as a tea, often taken during fevers as it produces profuse perspiration which cools down the body.

Take 3 or 4 leaves and place them in a pot; pour some boiling water over them and leave for a few minutes, then strain and sweeten.

## GINGER TEA

This is excellent for indigestion and stomach ache.

1 large piece of ginger, crushed        sugar
2½ cups (1 pint, 600 ml) water

Wash the ginger carefully and boil it in the water for a few minutes. Strain and sweeten to taste.

## CERASEE TEA

Cerasee (Momordica charantia) is a vine which produces fruit somewhat like the Chinese bitter melon or fooh gwaah. It grows wild in open lots and on fences. It is to be found in tropical and sub-tropical areas of both hemispheres. It is bitter and I wonder why it is so liked!

Boil about 1 oz (25 g) of cerasee in 2 cups (¾ pint, 500 ml) of water for a few minutes. Strain and sweeten. It is said to be good for stomach pains.

## SYRUP FOR A SORE THROAT

juice of 2 limes
¼ cup (2 fl oz, 50 ml) honey

⅛ cup (1 fl oz, 25 ml) white proof rum

Mix the ingredients together and store in a jar. Take a tablespoonful when needed.

## BISSY (KOLA NUT)

The kola nut (*Cola acuminata*) is a native of tropical West Africa, but is now cultivated in many other tropical countries. In its native habitat, the people chew it because it contains two stimulants, caffeine and theo-bromine. Kola or cola is used in the manufacture of several soft drinks.

This recipe is very good for the relief of stomach ache. I am not so sure that it works as an antidote for poison, as my grandfather maintained.

Grate 2 kola nuts and pour on enough white proof rum to cover them completely. Take 2 tablespoonfuls when needed, shaking the mixture very well beforehand.

## BUSH BATH

The bush bath is in fact like a sauna, having the same effect of inducing relaxation and drowsiness.

This recipe is taken from Caroline Sullivan's *Jamaica Cookery Book* (1893).

'2 quarts of water, leaves of the ackee, soursop, joint wood, pimento, cowfoot; sage, velvet bush, guava, Jack-in-the-bush, thistle, cerasee, elder, lime leaf, liquorice bush'

Boiling water is poured on to the bushes placed in a large tub with a board across for the patient to sit on. A blanket or other heavy cloth is thrown over the patient. The steam envelopes the patient, causing profuse sweating.

Caroline Sullivan says:

This bath is firmly believed in by all Jamaicans. In fact, it is considered absolutely necessary after fevers or other illnesses. Children in high fevers are lifted out of bed into this bath (first wetting the head with cold water), dried quickly and put back into bed and covered well. Soon after, the patient falls into a deep refreshing sleep, and the perspiration comes out freely.

# BIBLIOGRAPHY

## GENERAL BIBLIOGRAPHY

Adams, C. D., *Flowering Plants Of Jamaica*, University of the West Indies, Mona, 1972.

Ammar, Nellie, 'They Came from the Midde East', *Jamaica Journal*, Vol. 4, No. 1, March 1970.

Andrade, Jacob A., *A Record of the Jews in Jamaica*, Kingston, 1941.

Barrett, L., *The Sun and the Drum*, Heinemann Educational Books, 1976.

Beckford, William, *A Descriptive Account of the Island of Jamaica*, 2 vols., London, 1790.

Beckwith, Martha, *Jamaica Proverbs*, No. 6, Poughkeepsie (Vassar), 1925.

Beckwith, Martha, *Black Roadways – a Study of Jamaican Folklife*, Chapel Hill, 1929.

Belisario, *Sketches of Character of the Negro in Jamaica* (1837), No. 1.

Bethencourt, Cardozode, 'Notes on the Spanish and Portuguese Jews in the U.S.A., Dutch Guiana and B.W.I. during the 17th and 18th Centuries', *Pubs. of the Am. Jew. Hist. Soc.*, New York.

Black, Clinton, *History of Jamaica*, Collins-Sangster, 1979.

Blome, Richard, *Description of Jamaica*, London, 1672.

Bourne, Edward G. (1860–1908), 'The History and Determination of the Line of Demarcation Established by Pope Alexander VI between the Spanish and Portuguese Fields of Discovery and Colonization', *Pamphlet Am. Hist. Soc. Report*, 1891.

Bourne, Edward G., *Spain in America (1450–1580)*, New York and London, Harper & Bros., 1904.

Broughton, Dr, *Hortus Eastensis – a Catalogue of Exotic Plants*, St Jago de la Vega (Aikman), 1794.

Burney, James (1750–1821), *Buccaneers of America* (reprint of 1816 edition), London, Allen & Unwin, 1949.

Las Casas, Bartolomé de, *Historiadores de Indias*, ed. Serrano y Sanchez, Madrid, 1909.

Cassidy, F. G., *Jamaica Talk*, Macmillan Education, 1961.

Cassidy, F. G., *Dictionary of Jamaican English*, London, Cambridge University Press, 1967.

Centeno, A., *A Description of Jamaica*, 1644.

Cundall, Frank, and Pieterez, L., *Jamaica under the Spaniards*, Kingston, Institute of Jamaica, 1919.

Cundall, Frank, and Anderson, Izett, *Jamaica Proverbs and Sayings*, 2nd edition, Sangsters Bookstores, in association with the Irish University Press of Shannon, Ireland.

Danielson, Bengt, 'What Happened on the Bounty', London, Allen & Unwin.

Duerden, J. E., *Journal of the Institute of Jamaica*, Vol. 2, No. 4, p. 1 and Vol. 2, No. 5, p. 444.

Dunn, Richard S., *Sugar and Slavery – the Rise of the Planter Class in the English W. Indies (1624–1713)*, University of North Carolina, 1972.

Hall, Douglas, and Minz, Sidney, 'The Origins of the Jamaican Internal Market System', *Papers in Caribbean Anthropology – Yale University Publications in Anthropology*, No. 57.

Hall, Douglas, 'Bountied European Immigration into Jamaica with Reference to the German Settlement at Seaford Town to 1850', University of the West Indies, Mona.

Hurston, Zora Neale, *Voodoo Gods – an Inquiry into Native Myths and Magic in Jamaica and Haiti*, London, J. M. Dent & Son, 1939.

Labat, Jean-Baptiste (1663–1738), *Nouveau Voyage aux Antilles de L'Amérique*, 8 vols., Paris, T. Legras, 1722.

Leslie, Charles, *A New and Exact Account of Jamaica*, Edinburgh, Fleming, 1739.

Lewis, M. G., *Journal of a West Indian Proprietor*, London, 1834.

Lind, Andrew, 'Adjustment Patterns among the Jamaican Chinese', *Social and Economic Studies*, University of the West Indies, Mona, No. 7 (2), June (1959), 144:164.

Long, Edward, *History of Jamaica*, 3 vols., London, Lowndes, 1774.

Louen, Sven, *Origins of the Tianan Culture in the West Indies*, Goteborg Elanders Boktryckeri, Akitebolas, 1935.

MacFayden, James, *The Flora of Jamaica*, London, Longman, 1837.

Madden, R. R., *A Twelve Months Residence in the West Indies*, London, 1835.

Mansingh, Lakshmi and Ajai, 'Indian Heritage in Jamaica', *Jamaica Journal*, Vol. 10, Nos. 2, 3 and 4.

Mathewson, Duncan R., 'Archaeological Analysis of Material Culture as a Reflection of Sub-cultural Differentiation in 18th Century Jamaica', *Jamaica Journal*, Vol. 7, Nos. 1 and 2, March/June 1973.

Moreton, J. B., *Manners and Customs in the West Indies*, London, Richardson, Gardner & Walker, 1790.

Nugent, Lady, *Lady Nugents Journal of Her Residence in Jamaica from 1801 to 1805*, ed. Philip Wright, Institute of Jamaica, 1966.

Oviedo, Gonzalo Fernandez de (1478–1557), *Natural History of the West Indies* (translation), ed. S. A. Stoudemire, Chapel Hill, University of North Carolina Press, 1959.

Patterson, Orlando, *Sociology of Slavery*, London, 1967.

Phillipo, J., *Jamaica, its Past and Present*, London, 1843.

Renny, Robert, *An History of Jamaica – with Observations on the Climate . . .*, London, Cawthorn, 1807.

Rochefort, Charles de la, 'Histoire Naturelle et Morale des Iles Antilles de L'Amérique', Rotterdam, Jeers, 1658.

Rouse, Irving, *The Arawaks – Handbook of South American Indians*, Vol. 4, pp. 507–46.

Sloane, Hans, *A Voyage to the Islands, Madera, Barbados, Jamaica*, London, Vol. 1, 1707; Vol. 2, 1725.

Tertre, Jean du, *Histoire Générale des Antilles Habitée par les Francqis*, 1667–71.

Trapham, Thomas, *A Discourse on the State of Health in the Island of Jamaica*, London, 1679.

Trollope, Anthony, *The West Indies and the Spanish Main*, London, Chapman & Hall, 1860.

Wright, Irene A., *Early History of Cuba – 1492–1586*, New York, Macmillan, 1916.

## CARIBBEAN COOKERY BOOKS

Baille, Mrs W., *The Peter Pan Book of Recipes*, Kingston, 1929.

Brandon, Leila, *Merry Go Round of Recipes*, Kingston, 1963.

Clarendon, Ladies of, *A Taste of Jamaica*.

Clarke, E. Phillis, *West Indian Cookery*, London, Nelson, 1945.

Cleary, Teresa E., *Jamaica Run Dung*, Kingston, 1970.

Cook, Betty Ann (ed.), *Cookbook Ste Lucie*.

*Cooking of the Caribbean Islands*, Time Inc., Foods of the World series, 1970.

Grancher, Jacques (ed.), *Da Mathilde – 325 Recettes de Cuisine Creole*, Edition de la Pensée Moderne, Paris, 1975.

Grey, Winnifred, *Caribbean Cookery*, London, Collins, 1965.

Hawkes, Alex, *Rum Cookbook*, Collins-Sangster, Kingston, 1976.

Jamaica Information Service, *Banana Recipes*.

Krochmal, Connie and Arnold, *Caribbean Cookery*, Quadrangle, 1974.

Manville Fenn, Annie, *Housekeeping in Jamaica*, 16 March 1893.

Ortiz, Elizabeth L., *Caribbean Cooking*, Penguin, 1977.

St Lucia Tourist Board, *What's Cooking in St Lucia*.

Slater, Mary, *Caribbean Cooking for Pleasure*, Hamlyn, 1970.

Springer, Rita, *Caribbean Cookbook*, London, Evans, 1968.

Sullivan, Caroline, *Jamaica Cookery Book*, Kingston, Aston W. Gardner & Co., 1893.

# LIST OF U.K. SUPPLIERS

Most Asian-operated grocers and greengrocers carry food items used in Jamaican cooking, as do London street markets featuring 'ethnic' supplies, for example, Nags Head, Holloway, N7, Portobello Road, W11, and Brixton, SW9. Greek greengrocers' shops in Caledonian Road and Upper Street, London, N1, have some items available, and there is a concentration of shops between numbers 25 and 104 Stroud Green Road, London N4 (approaching the junction with Tollington Park), in which most items can be located.

Enco (London) Ltd, 71/5 Fortess Road, London NW5, imports all West Indian foods and, if you have difficulties finding any ingredients and write to them, they will give you the name of your nearest stockist from their list of some 4,000 retail outlets which are their customers.

Mrs A. Francis, Bull Ring Open Market, **Birmingham**
Mrs B. Spencer, Bull Ring Open Market, **Birmingham**
Mrs C. M. Tomlinson, Bull Ring Open Market, **Birmingham**
Dugal Grocers, 361 Dudley Road, Winston Green, **Birmingham**
Erdington Food Hall, 316 Slade Road, Erdington, **Birmingham**
Fresh Save, Handsworth Market, Soho Road, **Birmingham**
Sadiq Bros., 106 Soho Road, Handsworth, **Birmingham**
Poonia Super Market, 23/25 Birchfield Road, 6 Ways, Aston, **Birmingham**
Six Ways Fruit Hall, 118 Birchfield Road, 6 Ways, Aston, **Birmingham**
Continental Grocery Store, 46 Chelsea Road, Easton, **Bristol 5**
Mehta & Co., 163 Stoney Stanton Road, **Coventry**
B.B. Stores, 105 Barton Street, **Gloucester**
Mohamdie Store, 22/24 Rycroft Street, **Gloucester**
Barrard Stoke, 75 Broad Street, **Henley-on-Thames**
Caribbean Super Market, 45 St Stephens Road, **Leicester**
Caribbean Market (grocers), 69 Stroud Green Road, **London N4**
Star Cash and Carry, 68A Blackstock Road, **London N4**
Charlie's Tasties, 523 Seven Sisters Road, Tottenham, **London N15**
Oriental Grocers, 241 Camden High Street, **London NW1**
Europa Foods, 46 Englands Lane, **London NW3**
The Market, 271 Neasden Lane, Neasden, **London NW10**
Neasden Cash and Carry, 267 Neasden Lane, Neasden, **London NW10**

W. H. Roe & Son (wet and dry fishmongers), 12 Shepherd's Bush Market, London W12

Quality Stores, Devonshire Road, Chiswick, London W4

Ealing Food Store, Leelands Road, West Ealing, London W13

Eastern Emporium, 114 Acre Lane, London SW2

M. Adaz, 207 Coldharbour Lane, London SW9

Kaka Stores, 9 Sheep Street, Northampton

Johal Cash and Carry, 14 Cholmeley Road, Reading

Quality Fruiterers and Groceries, 90 Oxford Road, Reading

Rahman General Stores, 45 Cholmeley Road, Reading

A. Williams, 184 Oxford Road, Reading

Seema Super Store, 64/66 Craven Road, Rugby

S. H. Raja, 133/135 Spital Hill, Sheffield

Shah Oriental Grocers Ltd, 451/453 Abbey Dale Road, Sheffield

Lotte Super Market, 126 Malden Road, New Malden, Surrey

T. Singh, Stall 567, Market Hall, Slope Street, Wolverhampton

Bill Williams, Stall 40, Open Market, Wolverhampton

# Index